A Facing History and Ourselves Publication

What Do We Do with a Difference?
France and the Debate over Headscarves in Schools

With an Introduction by John R. Bowen

FACING
HISTORY
AND
OURSELVES

Facing History and Ourselves is an international educational and professional development organization whose mission is to engage students of diverse backgrounds in an examination of racism, prejudice, and antisemitism in order to promote the development of a more humane and informed citizenry. By studying the historical development of the Holocaust and other examples of genocide, students make the essential connections between history and the moral choices they confront in their own lives. For more information about Facing History and Ourselves, please visit our website at *www.facinghistory.org.*

Cover art photo: © AP Photo/François Mori

To receive additional copies of this resource, please visit *www.facinghistory.org/publications.*

ISBN-13: 978-0-9798440-4-1
ISBN-10: 0-9798440-4-5

FACING
HISTORY
AND
OURSELVES

Facing History and Ourselves Headquarters
16 Hurd Road
Brookline, MA 02445-6919

ABOUT FACING HISTORY AND OURSELVES

Facing History and Ourselves is a nonprofit educational organization whose mission is to engage students of diverse backgrounds in an examination of racism, prejudice, and antisemitism in order to promote a more humane and informed citizenry. As the name Facing History and Ourselves implies, the organization helps teachers and their students make the essential connections between history and the moral choices they confront in their own lives, and offers a framework and a vocabulary for analyzing the meaning and responsibility of citizenship and the tools to recognize bigotry and indifference in their own worlds. Through a rigorous examination of the failure of democracy in Germany during the 1920s and '30s and the steps leading to the Holocaust, along with other examples of hatred, collective violence, and genocide in the past century, Facing History and Ourselves provides educators with tools for teaching history and ethics, and for helping their students learn to combat prejudice with compassion, indifference with participation, and myth and misinformation with knowledge.

Believing that no classroom exists in isolation, Facing History and Ourselves offers programs and materials to a broad audience of students, parents, teachers, civic leaders, and all of those who play a role in the education of young people. Through significant higher education partnerships, Facing History and Ourselves also reaches and impacts teachers before they enter their classrooms.

By studying the choices that led to critical episodes in history, students learn how issues of identity and membership, ethics and judgment have meaning today and in the future. Facing History and Ourselves' resource books provide a meticulously researched yet flexible structure for examining complex events and ideas. Educators can select appropriate readings and draw on additional resources available online or from our comprehensive lending library.

Our foundational resource book, *Facing History and Ourselves: Holocaust and Human Behavior*, embodies a sequence of study that begins with identity—first individual identity and then group and national identities, with their definitions of membership. From there the program examines the failure of democracy in Germany and the steps leading to the Holocaust—the most documented case of twentieth-century indifference, de-humanization, hatred, racism, antisemitism, and mass murder. It goes on to explore difficult questions of judgment, memory and legacy, and the necessity for responsible participation to prevent injustice. Facing History and Ourselves then returns to the theme of civic participation to examine stories of individuals, groups, and nations who have worked to build just and inclusive communities and whose stories illuminate the courage, compassion, and political will that are needed to protect democracy today and in generations to come. Other examples in which civic dilemmas test democracy, such as the Armenian genocide and the U.S. civil rights movement, expand and deepen the connection between history and the choices we face today and in the future.

Facing History and Ourselves has offices or resource centers in the United States, Canada, and the United Kingdom as well as in-depth partnerships in Rwanda, South Africa, and Northern Ireland. Facing History and Ourselves' outreach is global, with educators trained in more than 80 countries and delivery of our resources through a website accessed worldwide with online content delivery, a program for international fellows, and a set of NGO partnerships. By convening conferences of scholars, theologians, educators, and journalists, Facing History and Ourselves' materials are kept timely, relevant, and responsive to salient issues of global citizenship in the twenty-first century.

For more than 30 years, Facing History and Ourselves has challenged students and educators to connect the complexities of the past to the moral and ethical issues of today. They explore democratic values and consider what it means to exercise one's rights and responsibilities in the service of a more humane and compassionate world. They become aware that "little things are big"—seemingly minor decisions can have a major impact and change the course of history.

For more about Facing History and Ourselves, visit our website at *www.facinghistory.org*.

Acknowledgments

Primary Writer: Dan Eshet

Series Editor: Adam Strom

Writing *What Do We Do with a Difference?: France and the Debate over Headscarves in Schools* has been a team effort. As we worked on this project, the team engaged in profound conversations about identity, belonging, religion, and citizenship. Direction about the project's scope, themes, and particular resources came from discussions among Facing History and Ourselves' staff, teachers, scholars, and friends.

We deeply appreciate the contributions of Mark Kingdon, who provided support and challenged us to create resources that would help Facing History reach new audiences and teach about the civic dilemmas of our age. Adam Strom, Director of Research and Development, led the project, and Dan Eshet wrote the text. Nadia Gaber, Aliza Landes, and Ido Gabay provided key research along the way. Cameron Fryer and Jennifer Gray did wonderful photo research to bring these stories to life. Nicole Breaux, the project manager, made sure all the elements came together in a timely manner. The leadership of Margot Stern Strom, Executive Director, and Marc Skvirsky, Chief Program Officer, made this project possible; together they made numerous thoughtful contributions to the text. Marty Sleeper also read the text and provided valuable feedback and editorial suggestions. Sam Gilbert and Josephine Roccuzzo were very thorough editors, and Brown Publishing Network created the page design and tenaciously reviewed the final pages. We would also like to thank Catherine O'Keefe, Luisa Ehrich, and Robert Lavelle, without whom our text would remain a Word document. Joe Battaglia designed lessons to help teachers bring this resource into the classroom. Francesca Tramboulakis helped us secure permissions for publications.

Facing History and Ourselves would like to thank John Bowen for his thoughtful introduction; his book *Why the French Don't Like Headscarves* sparked a number of fruitful discussions about this material. Professors Daniel Cohen, Zvi Ben-Dor, and Jonathan Laurence taught us so much as we researched the French headscarf debate; we cannot thank them enough for their support. There are a number of others whose contributions deserve special recognition, among them Adrianne Billingham Bock, Alan Stoskopf, Amy Beckhusen, Anna Romer, Dennis Barr, Diane Moore, Dimitry Anselme, Doc Miller, Elisabeth Kanner, Frank Buijs, Jack Weinstein, Jose Casanova, Joy Lei, Juan Castellanos, Jean-Louis Auduc, Judy Wise, Karen Murphy, Martha Minow, Steven Becton, Laura Tavares, Phyllis Goldstein, Riem Spielhaus, Viola Georgi, Zainab Al-Suwaij, Jeremy Nesoff, and Jessica Bowen.

"In France the national and republican projects have been identified with a certain idea of citizenship. This French idea of the nation and republic by nature respects all convictions, particularly religious and political beliefs and cultural traditions. But it rules out the breaking down of the nation into separate communities which are indifferent to one another. . . . The nation is not only a group of citizens who hold individual rights. It is a community with a [common] destiny. . . . This secular and national ideal is the very substance of the republican school and the foundation of its duty of civic education."

— *François Bayrou, French Minister of Education*

"Perhaps it's the democratic outcomes I'm interested in more than the principle of secularism itself."

— *Joan Wallach Scott, American scholar*

Table of Contents

Preface

By Adam Strom
Director of Research and Development
Facing History and Ourselves

"The histories taught through Facing History and Ourselves show very clearly how categorizing people into groups has been used as the basis for segregation, apartheid, and genocide."

How we define who is like "us" and who is not is an issue of extraordinary importance and consequence. Often rooted in the complex process of individual identity formation, questions of sameness and difference take on greater significance when applied to groups and nations. Some argue that categorizing people into groups is natural and part of the way humans try to make sense of their world. In defining identity, people consider what differences between people should matter. For example, should skin color, culture, or national origin be markers of identity? What about differences in gender, religion, or sexual orientation? How should people decide which differences to emphasize and what to do with those differences?

These conversations are essential to Facing History and Ourselves. The scope and sequence of resources, seminars, and workshops begin with vital conversations about individual identity and the ways in which one component of how we define ourselves, especially for adolescents, is how we think we are defined by others—a dynamic which is basic to the relationship between the individual and society. While making and categorizing differences may be natural, some scholars warn that misuse can lead to hatred and mass violence. The histories taught through Facing History and Ourselves reveal how categorizing people as "other" has been used as the basis for segregation, apartheid, and genocide. Studying these histories will promote essential questions about citizenship, integration, and the consequences of how individuals, groups, and nations define their collective identities.

In our globalized world, each of us finds ourself—in big and small ways—living with differences. Migration and immigration are the most visible examples. That is where this book begins. With record numbers of migrants moving across the world, how will communities respond? How will they define who is a "we" and who is not? And how do myths, misinformation, and stereotypes influence those decisions? Debates about national identity and the goals of integration have become headline topics in a number of countries around the world, where policymakers face the dilemma of how to reinforce national bonds while at the same time respecting religious and cultural differences.

This book focuses on the recent debates surrounding headscarves in public schools in France, where the wearing of an article of clothing became the focus of intense national debate. Why did people begin to view the headscarf as infringing on the principle of secularity and other French values? And how did it threaten national identity? To explore these questions, we turn to history. The challenge of balancing group identity with integration is acutely felt in Western European countries such as France, Germany, the United Kingdom, and the Netherlands, where large populations of immigrants have settled during the decades of recovery from the devastation of World War II. Immigration into these countries not only altered their ethnic and religious composition, but also upset the national consensus about the values, traditions, and identities their citizens share. As a result, each of these countries must inevitably examine and perhaps reassess its immigration and integration policies. The efforts to integrate diverse populations often raise questions about how far societies should go to accommodate minorities. In this book we call these questions "civic dilemmas."

In Europe, much of the discussion in recent years has focused on the treatment of an increasingly visible Muslim population. Islam, to which many immigrants subscribe, has also become the lightning rod for discussions about the place of religion in Europe's secular societies. French scholar Olivier Roy warns us that the debates say as much about the identities of the host societies as they do about Muslims in Europe. As Roy explains, "Islam is a mirror in which the West projects its own identity crisis."[1]

How should individuals, groups, and nations respond to religious differences? Part of the answer to this question lies in the way different nations define secularity. In the United States, the first amendment to the Constitution promises both freedom from state religion and freedom of religious expression. In contrast, in an effort to create a space where all individuals are treated equally, the French civic or public sphere is a space free of religious influence—it is a religiously neutral arena, where republican, universal ideals rule. In recent years, however, some have suggested that this "universal civic space" does not allow for all people, especially observant Muslims, to express fundamental aspects of their identity. These issues raise profound questions about how free of religious influence European culture really is—when, for example, calendars and customs still reflect Europe's Christian heritage. What is the relationship between secularity and democracy? Or, more pointedly, does the pursuit of secularity conflict with the pursuit of democracy?

In this book we trace how a local incident involving Islamic head coverings sparked a global discussion about integration. The conversations were fueled by often unspoken assumptions about Islam, secularity, violence, and national identity. These assumptions make all the difference: they influence the choices people make about who's in and who's out, and to whom the nation extends full rights and privileges. We have chosen to focus on the debate in France, a country proud of its republican traditions emphasizing assimilation as a path of acceptance. The French case study illuminates what is at stake as a nation negotiates its identity in the midst of the dilemmas individuals and groups face as they work to create a sustainable and safe civic space for all inhabitants.

This book is composed of two main parts. The first part is an essay that provides background and analysis of the veil affairs in France, the history of the North African immigrants there, and the hopes and struggles of their descendants (the so-called second and third generation). The second part provides readings that are primary documents designed to be used by teachers in the classroom to expand and highlight the main points covered in the essay. Sources include images, speeches, interviews, and song lyrics. The documents offer a wide range of opinions on identity and belonging and on the implications of the headscarf debate in France.

Facing History and Ourselves believes that educators can meet the challenges of teaching in this global age, in which we live increasingly in communities with people whose appearance, experiences, and traditions strike us as different from our own. Decades of classroom experience have taught us that avoiding these issues will not make them disappear. Indeed, silence may leave a space that can be filled by prejudice, fear, and misunderstanding. It is the role of educators to help students confront cultural differences and recognize themselves in other people's stories.

The present study of the headscarves debate in France offers several ways to open valuable dialogues with students about the meaning of integration. Considered together, the essay and the readings that follow present a paradox that is at the heart of education in a globalized world. In their book *Just Schools: Pursuing Equality in Societies of Difference*, scholars Martha Minow, Richard A. Shweder, and Hazel Rose Markus summarize the situation:

> The challenge of promoting just schooling in a diverse society presents us with what can be called the equality-difference paradox: a tension between, on the one side, social and political efforts to advance equality for all regardless of culture, religion, race, or class, and government support for pluralism and multiculturalism on the other. Do schools promote integration along the lines of race, ethnicity, religion, and economic class, or instead divide students along these or other lines? Do schools with diverse student bodies encourage the development of one common identity or instead foster distinctive group identities—and which of these avenues better expands opportunities or confers respect on the individuals involved?[2]

The ability to answer these questions could make the difference between fostering a tolerant and egalitarian society and allowing communities to slip into conflicts, violence, and even acts of terror. We hope that this essay and the documents that follow it help teachers anticipate and reduce such tensions.

This book raises powerful questions for educators, who often struggle with the question of how to teach students common values and national solidarity while also respecting their diverse needs and cultural backgrounds. By focusing on the ways that young adults and students are prepared to live together in an increasingly pluralistic society, we hope that this case study will also shed light on the role of education in integrating minorities in countries well beyond the French borders.

Key Questions:

1. How should nations recognize newcomers' cultures and identities? How can they facilitate their peaceful integration? Will banning a religious symbol make a country more or less democratic?

2. When do religious symbols take on a political meaning?

3. How can educators reconcile the need to treat people *equally*, the need to treat people *differently*, and the need to cultivate a *shared sense of belonging*?

4. What skills do citizens need to be able to participate in an informed discussion about immigration and national identity with people whose backgrounds and politics are different from their own?

---

[1] Olivier Roy, *Secularism Confronts Islam*, trans. George Holoch (New York: Columbia University Press, 2007), xiii.

[2] Martha Minow, Richard A. Shweder, and Hazel Rose Markus (eds.), *Just Schools: Pursuing Equality in Societies of Difference* (New York: Russell Sage Foundation, 2008), 5–6.

Introduction

By John R. Bowen
Dunbar-Van Cleve Professor of Art and Science
Washington University, St. Louis

At least for a few months during 2004 and 2005, France got more than its usual share of the world's attention. First, in early 2004, nearly everyone in French public life rallied around a law making it illegal for Muslim girls to wear Islamic headscarves to public schools. In fact the law was written to prohibit any signs that drew clear attention to one's religion, but it was aimed at Muslim girls. It is rare enough that the Left and Right agree on anything in France, but they seemed united in their displeasure at this particular choice of couture.

And then, in the fall of 2005, riots broke out in many of France's poor outer cities, the *banlieues*. Some of the young people living in the tall, isolated housing projects had become so angry about the 50% youth unemployment, police harassment, and lack of much in the way of entertainment that they burned cars and torched buildings. The country seemed to be falling apart, and people were excited about headscarves? What was going on?

In the book you are about to read, you will discover the background to these events in the histories of immigration, the meanings of secularity (*laïcité*), acts of antisemitism and racism, and, most importantly, the songs and stories and sentiments of the people most affected: daughters and sons of those who came from Muslim-majority societies, mainly in North Africa, to help rebuild France after World War II. Some of those children of immigrants, the so-called Beur generation—and now *their* children—regret that their parents' sacrifices were not followed up by a full and fraternal welcome from those "native French" whose motto celebrates liberty, equality, and fraternity. This regret, and not a desire to build Islamic ghettos, lay behind the riots of 2005 and behind the discontent that still simmers.

A complex series of political stunts, ponderous deliberations, media exaggerations, and serious studies eventually led to the banning of young girls' headscarves. (Calling them "the veil" makes these lightweight bits of chiffon seem more threatening than even French teachers ever thought them to be.) But once we have come to understand what happened, what do we make of it? Do we tell the French to shape up and read the United States Constitution? Do we ask the United States Department of State to put France on a blacklist for denying religious freedom? Maybe we should bring out "freedom fries" one more time?

Although I have been quite critical of how French public figures went about drumming up support for the law, my argument was that some in France were not acting consistently with their *own* principles, not that they needed to adopt someone else's. French republicanism rests on a set of principles about how a nation holds together. Not all versions of these principles agree with each other, and France has made compromises along the way that make republicanism-in-practice quite different from republicanism-in-theory, but principles they are. In the French view of things, people develop into citizens by abstracting from their particular religious identities or cultural practices a set of common beliefs and values—in human equality, for example, or in the value of electoral democracy. They are supposed to bring these foundations for a common life into their social interactions and into political life—and leave the rest at home.

How do they learn to think and live in this way? At least since the end of the nineteenth century, the republican answer has been (in principle) simple: get the Catholic Church out of public life, and put all children into centralized public schools. But implementing this program was far from simple. The Vatican said no, and even if it had no army, Rome had foot soldiers—thousands of French citizens ready and able to descend into the streets and bring down governments. By the 1950s, decades of negotiations (and a few of those massive demonstrations) had produced a compromise that has lasted relatively well: Catholics could run their own schools, and the state would even pay their teachers' salaries if they would teach the same curriculum as in the secular schools. A few Jewish schools followed suit, and today about one-half of French families make some use of a private school (for 95% of them a Catholic school) at some time. Along the way, the state agreed that it or municipal governments would keep the church buildings going, as well.

Few in France wish to reopen or upset this rather delicate package of compromises. But neither are many people happy about injecting a new religion into the mix, one whose spokespersons feel perfectly in the right when they request state aid to pay *their* religious-school teachers and help build *their* places of worship. That this new religion is Islam has made things worse, because the rise in these requests for equal treatment at home has come just at the time when many in Europe have become more and more worried about global political Islam.

To some degree, French public officials have recognized that Muslim demands for mosques and schools are fair, if not entirely welcome, and government aid has been forthcoming. But the French state sticks to a rather strict notion of what is and what is not protected as "religious practice" in France. If the faithful have a right to worship in decent places, to teach their credos, to eat kosher or halâl food, and certainly (see the *Declaration of the Rights of Man*) to think religious thoughts, their constitutionally protected rights stop at the church door, so to speak. Most French officials and intellectuals, on the Left or the Right, consider it a civic imperative to keep public life free of divisive credos. This imperative justifies forbidding civil servants (teachers, postal workers, nurses) from wearing anything that might indicate their religious preference, and keeping "religious signs" out of public schools—and especially when some see Islamic headscarves as signifying the subordination of women in Islam and the dangers of global Islamism. In this view, ensuring that everyone lives a common life on shared principles should take precedence over claims by individuals that they should be free to practice their religion in public spaces.

How does this approach play out in Europe, where the European Court of Human Rights is charged with ensuring that everyone is free to "manifest his religion" either in private or in public? Well, the relevant text—Article 9 of the European Convention on Human Rights—also allows states to limit this right for the protection of "public order," morals, and the rights of others, and the Court has given states considerable maneuvering room in defining what these protections require. There is no single European perspective on this issue—and should there be?

The issue is moral and philosophical before it is legal. Consider one small example. In 2003, filmmaker Micah Fink filmed a PBS documentary on life at a *lycée* south of Paris. He followed a pupil who wore a scarf through her struggle with the school. He interviewed the school principal, as well, but we see her subjectivity next to that of the girl, and the liberal response that follows most easily from learning of these juxtaposed subjectivities is to say: let a hundred flowers bloom. It is hard to view the program without concluding: "good Muslims, reasonable principal, but intolerant state."

The principal of the school saw the issue quite differently. She mentioned another Muslim pupil in her school who did not fast or wear a headscarf, and who might have felt pressure had there not been a ban on scarf-wearing or fast-breaking in school. As she told me: "There is pressure within the school on girls. I want to make sure that people are free to decide on their own about dress, prayer, fasting, and so forth." If the American insistence on freedom of choice *assumes* the possibility of choosing, and thus sees the matter as a private one, the French emphasis on autonomy and dignity sees it as the state's obligation to take steps to *create the conditions* for meaningful choice. From that perspective, "choice" appears as a naively thin concept.

I find both the liberal approach and the republican one to be reasonable visions of political life, even if I disagree with how France approached the headscarves question. Each of these visions respects a set of basic, important political concepts, which include choice, freedom of religion, autonomy, and civic unity. They differ in the order of priority they give to these four concepts: a liberal approach (as practiced in England, for example) places the first two concepts higher than the next two without denying the value of any; a republican approach (as in France) turns the order around. This overall way of looking at differences in moral and political visions is the European one: allow for reasonable differences, but hold the line on basic principles of human rights and justice.

But we may still exercise our right to offer critiques of particular decisions and solutions to these questions, and, I think, these critiques are most effective when we make them *within* a particular moral and political vision. We might then say, not "How can you deny a basic right to these girls?" but "Could visible religious differences be a tool for teaching civic unity rather than its implacable foe?"

Timeline

1789–1799:

- The French Revolution. During this political and social upheaval, the "Third Estate" (the common people) overturns the French monarchy and establishes a revolutionary government based on the principles of popular sovereignty. France's revolutionary government expropriates vast properties owned by the church, the aristocracy, and the nobility and distributes them among the peasantry. With "liberty, equality, and fraternity" as its slogan, the French Revolution became an inspirational model for future democratic revolutions. Some trace the origins of French secularity to this event.

- A new regime, based on the principles of popular sovereignty and the inalienable rights of all citizens, begins to emerge. The Revolution's slogan of "liberté, égalité, fraternité" (French for "liberty, equality, brotherhood") becomes the motto of France's future democratic governments (known successively as "Republics").

- During the Revolution, in 1791, Jews are emancipated—they receive full civic rights as individuals, but none as a group. This formula provides the blueprint for the assimilation of all ethnic groups in France for the next two centuries.

1830:

The foundation of French colonialism is laid when France invades North Africa and, in the next decades, occupies Algeria, Tunisia, and Morocco. France also expands its empire deep into areas in western and central Africa.

1881–1882:

The Jules Ferry Laws establish mandatory, free, and secular (*laïque*) education for all French students under the age of 15. Ferry, the education minister behind these laws, is credited with two critical achievements:

1) The creation of a national culture that unified France's disparate vernaculars and local traditions.

2) The establishment of a secular education system that relied on state-paid professional teachers rather than on the Catholic clerics who were perceived as an obstacle to the democratic process in France.

1894–1906:

The Dreyfus Affair. In 1894, Alfred Dreyfus, a Jewish military officer, is arrested and accused of selling secrets to the Germans. The false accusations and the public debates surrounding his trial draw attention to deep-seated antisemitism in France, which had persisted long after the Jews were granted equal civil liberties in 1791. In 1906, after 12 years and massive public protests, Dreyfus is exonerated and is restored to his military post.

1905:

A French law on the separation of church and state is passed on December 9, 1905. The law is regarded as the legal foundation of France's secularity (*laïcité*).

1939–1945:

World War II. France is occupied by the German Third Reich. The Nazi-controlled Vichy government actively participates in the deportation of close to 75,000 of the 300,000 Jews who live in France to Nazi concentration camps, where most of them perished.

1945–1973:

Les Trente Glorieuses ("the glorious thirty [years]"). During the three decades following the end of World War II, France and other European nations experience spectacular economic growth. Hundreds of thousands of North African laborers are brought as "guest workers" to serve in the booming economy, which ends abruptly in 1973.

1954–1962:

The Algerian War. The use of indiscriminate violence, torture, and terror leaves deep scars in the national memory of both France and Algeria. It sets the tone for decades of complicated and often tense relations between France and its former colonies.

1962:

The Évian Agreements are signed by France and Algeria, putting an end to the Algerian War and the French colonial enterprise there. The agreements restart the pre-war immigration from North Africa, and many "guest workers" are again recruited to serve in France's most grueling jobs. Similar agreements secure the inflow of immigrants from other former colonies.

1972:

A veteran of the Algerian war, Jean-Marie Le Pen, forms the National Front, a far-right nationalistic party. Capitalizing on and fueling anti-immigrant sentiments (directed especially against Jewish immigrants from Arab countries), Le Pen repeatedly runs for president, with his support peaking in the 2002 elections.

1973–1974:

Sparked by the Yom Kippur War between Israel and its Arab neighbors, an international oil crisis begins in 1973. It leads to a severe downturn in the European economy. To fight high rates of unemployment, France attempts to tighten immigration laws, although family reunification policies (and illegal immigration) contribute to a steady flow of foreigners into France.

1979:

After civic unrest forces out Iranian Shah Mohammad Reza Pahlavi, Ruhollah Khomeini comes back from exile and installs an Islamic government. Khomeini enforces harsh censorship, strict religious laws, and the wearing of the chador by all women. People suspected of dissent are routinely arrested and some are executed by a special military branch called the Islamic Revolution's Guards. The regime's policies reinforce the negative perception of Islam in the minds of many in the West.

1981:

François Mitterrand is elected as the first socialist president of the French Republic. His election marks a change in the public perception of ethnic diversity. For several years, France celebrates its ethnic and religious groups.

Timeline (continued)

1983:

The "March of the Beurs" draws tens of thousands of supporters in Paris. During the march, the Beurs, descendants of Arab immigrants, protest the violence and discrimination directed against them. The march marks the coming of age of the Beurs as a group; it also focuses public discussion on the question of ethnicity.

1989:

- France celebrates the bicentennial of the French Revolution.

- Iranian leader Ayatollah Ruhollah Khomeini issues a decree (*fatwa* in Arabic) calling for the death of Salman Rushdie, an Indian-British author who published a controversial novel entitled *The Satanic Verses*. The decree engenders fear of the spread of Islamic fundamentalism.

- The first national "veil affair" unfolds in a public school in Creil, a town north of Paris, where three Muslim French girls (of North African descent) refuse to take off their headscarves in school. While many schools continue to accommodate veiled girls, others protest what they view as a violation of the principle of secularity.

- France's highest administrative court, the Conseil d'État, rules that the veil is compatible with the French separation of church and state.

- The fall of the Berlin Wall symbolizes the end of the Cold War. Talks of deeper European cooperation raise the prospect of Turkey's integration into the European Union and the integration of Muslim immigrants, whose identity is seen by many as irreconcilable with Europe's.

1993:

The "Pasqua Law," named after the French interior minister Charles Pasqua, is enacted in an effort to stop the immigration flow into France. Anti-immigrant sentiments (directed especially against immigrants from North African/Arab countries) are on the rise as the Muslim population begins to build its community's institutions and become visible.

1994:

Minister of Education François Bayrou issues a memorandum banning the veil (and other "ostentatious" religious symbols) in public schools. Despite the memorandum, Muslim girls continue to come to school wearing the veil, spurring new local and, occasionally, national debates about religion in public schools.

1995:

- The Armed Islamic Group, an Algerian Islamist organization, expands its armed struggle against the Algerian secular government into France. Attacks in Paris and Lyon leave eight people dead and injure more than 100. The terror attacks create widespread fear and contribute to the perception of Islam as a violent religion.

- Jacques René Chirac is elected president of the French Republic.

1999:

Two girls of Turkish origin are expelled from a public junior high school in the town of Flers (in northwest France) after a teachers' strike protesting veiling in school.

2001:

On September 11, 2001, 19 members of the Islamic-jihadist organization al-Qaeda in the United States hijack four airplanes and crash them into the World Trade Center in New York and the Pentagon in Washington, D.C. Close to 3,000 people are killed in these suicide attacks.

2002–2004:

An increase in antisemitic attacks in France renews fears for the safety of Jews. The rise in anti-immigrant rhetoric leads to an increase in anti-Muslim attacks and to a peak in Le Pen's popularity. He finishes second in the first run in the presidential elections.

2003:

- The French Council of the Muslim Faith (Conseil Français du Culte Musulman) is established. This umbrella institution is formed with the goal of bringing Islam into the political process by recognizing it, alongside Catholicism, Protestantism, and Judaism, as one of the organized religions in France.

- President Chirac nominates Bernard Stasi to head a commission of 20 experts (the "Stasi Commission") to investigate the application of the principle of secularity (laïcité) in France and the best ways to protect it in the public sphere. Of all Stasi Commission recommendations, President Chirac asks the French legislature to adopt the suggestion to ban "ostentatious" religious symbols in public schools. The recommendation is widely seen as directed against the Islamic veil.

- During the Stasi Commission deliberation, the "Lévy Sister Affair" breaks when two high school students in the Henri-Wallon high school in the Parisian suburb of Aubervillers

refuse to lower their veils according to their school's rules. Daughters of a secular Algerian mother and an atheist-Jewish father, the two sisters are expelled from school.

2004:

- On March 11, 2004, an al-Qaeda-inspired terrorist cell orchestrates a series of attacks on the Madrid commuter train system, killing 191 people and injuring more than 1,700.

- On March 15, 2004, President Jacques Chirac signs a law banning the display of large religious symbols in public schools. The law, widely understood as a ban on the Islamic veil, is supported by a majority of the French public.

2005:

- On July 7, 2005, four militant Islamist suicide bombers strike in central London, killing 52 people and injuring 770.

- In October 2005, the banlieues of Paris and other French cities see unprecedented riots, violence, and arson. The rioters, most of them second- or third-generation children of Muslim immigrants from North Africa, protest against high rates of poverty, unemployment, and racism in the suburbs (banlieues in French).

2007:

Nicolas Sarkozy, of Hungarian and Greek Jewish descent, is elected president of the French Republic after a campaign that focuses on law and order and economic development. Despite tough talk, Sarkozy engages the Muslim population in politics and promotes "positive discrimination" (known in America as affirmative action) for immigrants.

Part One

Framing the Discussion

Essay: Immigration and Integration in Europe

" . . . [M]igrants and strangers, anthropologists warn us, don't come with labels; instead they are often **made into** *a minority by a majority that lays claim to the social or national 'we.'"*

Reports on mounting anti-immigrant sentiments in Europe have filled the electronic and printed media in the past few years. These reports, critics argue, center on Muslims who, in the minds of many Europeans, cannot (or will not) assimilate. While there is a lot of talk about a need for integration, for some Europeans, immigrant Muslims stand for everything that has gone wrong with immigration in the past few decades. Accused of backwardness, religious fanaticism, and incapacity to fit in, Muslims are often targeted by private individuals and public policies. Extremists have even suggested transferring the Muslim immigrants and their offspring back to their "home countries." How have Western European countries, who vowed to firm up their democracies and eradicate xenophobia in the aftermath of the Holocaust, found themselves in this position?

Complicating these issues are Islamist extremists who reject many aspects of Western culture, and the fear of home-grown terrorists (especially after the brutal attacks between 2001 and 2005 in the Unites States, London, and Madrid, which shattered the sense of security in the West). These issues influence the perception of Muslims in the West and lead many to conclude that they will never fit in. In this charged atmosphere, the dialogue between host communities and immigrants is carried out only irregularly and is often infused with tensions and preconceived notions. But

negotiating the differences between these communities is imperative. If these issues remain unresolved, if prejudices and suspicions prevail, Muslims are very likely to become Europe's new outcasts.[1] A series of urgent questions is therefore on the table: What reasonable expectations can nations place on minorities and immigrants? How much of the national values and cultures should immigrants be expected to adopt? And what changes need to be made to the national culture so that integration of legal immigrants is carried out peacefully?

The essay below and the readings that follow provide an in-depth analysis of France's recent attempts to integrate immigrants of Muslim background. In this book, we follow Facing History and Ourselves' familiar methodology: turning to history, we try to study the particularities of this case in order to reflect on its universal implications. As the name of our organization implies, history also provides us with insights into the choices and dilemmas we face in our own communities. This book is part of a new Facing History and Ourselves project that focuses on civic dilemmas. Both the project and the book examine the ways in which European countries attempt to reconcile their views about their secular political culture and the cultural and religious expectations of immigrants—particularly the growing Muslim minority. In the past two decades, the tensions between Europe's public culture and the needs of certain religious minorities have spurred heated debates on all continents. These debates touch upon the role of religion in democratic societies, the meaning of secularism, the questions of dual loyalties, and—especially—the role of education in preparing new citizens.

Migration has been a constant throughout human history; though the flow has waxed and waned, every society around the world has experienced the effects of displacement. Many scholars insist that the idea of ethnic or national purity is a myth—with the exception of very small communities, every group is heterogeneous. Moreover, migrants and strangers, anthropologists warn us, don't come with labels; instead they are often *made into* a minority by a majority that lays claim to the social or national "we." In modern societies, immigration laws and social practices shape the minority experience: these practices can be used to define the new arrivals as illegal "aliens," as "racially" inferior, or as outcasts. Attributes of these groups—the texture of their hair, the scent of their cuisine, their customary approach to resolving problems—are then transformed into negative qualities, a politicized process through which the stranger becomes undesirable, a target of scorn, at worst a victim of violence, even genocide, as history teaches us.[2]

For centuries, Europe sent more emigrants out into foreign lands than any other continent.[3] When the European countries began to build nation-states, the outward migration contributed to the perception that their nations were homogeneous: France was the home of the French, Britain of the Britons. Difference existed elsewhere.

The past few decades have revolutionized these assumptions in several ways. In the first place, these decades saw dramatic changes in the volume and pace of international migration. The number of migrants around the world today is staggering: There are over 190 million immigrants worldwide; in Asia, there are well over 50 million immigrants, 64 million in Europe, and 44 million in North America.[4] Immigration therefore has had a worldwide impact, but it seems most acutely felt in Europe. While attempts were made to slow the inflow of immigrants in the decades following the oil crisis of 1973, more than 8 percent—possibly as much as 10 percent—of the European population is now of non-European descent.

For example, a 2006 United Nations report suggests that more than 12 percent of the German population is foreign-born, that in France foreign-born residents make up roughly 10 percent of the total population, and that in Switzerland immigrants account for close to 23 percent of the local population (see chart).[6]

But immigration did not just change in size and pace. Since the end of World War II, the direction of global migration has been reversed and the West is now its primary recipient. In fact, immigration from countries in Africa, the Middle East, Asia, and South America into economically developed countries in the West is one of the most visible signs of our time. But although the number of immigrants to Europe has lately climbed to record heights, until recently, few Swedes or Frenchmen, for example, saw themselves as part of immigrant societies. And another change in recent decades: western and northern Europe have experienced very low birth rates among the traditional European population. Against this background, higher birth rates among immigrants raise fears that Europe's his-

Migrants in Various Countries

Country or Area	Total Population (thousands)	Migrant Stock		Net Migration (average annual)	
		Number (thousands)	Percentage of Population	Number (thousands)	Rate per 1,000 Population
	2005			2000-2005	
World	6,464,750	190,634	2.9	0	0.0
Northern Africa	190,895	1,838	1.0	-294	-1.6
Europe	728,389	64,116	8.8	1,083	1.5
Algeria	32,854	242	0.7	-20	-0.6
Morocco	31,479	132	0.4	-80	-2.6
Tunisia	10,103	38	0.4	-4	-0.4
United Kingdom	59,668	5,408	9.1	137	2.3
France	**60,496**	**6,471**	**10.7**	**60**	**1.002**
Germany	82,689	10,144	12.3	220	2.7
Netherlands	16,299	1,638	10.1	30	1.9
Switzerland	7,252	1,660	22.9	8	1.1
Denmark	5,431	389	7.2	12	2
Sweden	9,041	1,117	12.4	31	3.5
Turkey	73,193	1,328	1.8	-50	-0.7

Immigrants in Europe now make up 10 percent of the population. In North Africa, they make up less than one percent.
Source: Department of Economic and Social Affairs: Population Division.[5]

toric culture will die out.[7]

Moreover, contemporary immigration is accompanied by other exchanges—the back-and-forth flow of ideas, commodities, languages, and traditions—on scales that are astounding. To mark the scale and pace of this process, scholars and commentators have given it a name—globalization. Globalization has made our world smaller in one sense: regions that were beyond our reach (and even our imagination) just a few decades ago are now easily accessible by land, sea, or air. But our world has also become much bigger: we've become connected to regions, cultures, and people from the farthest corners of the world. This dynamic process is driven by economics—by the creation of multina-

tional companies, by the search for new markets across the globe, and by the creation of electronic networks that tie this global system together. Immigration is central to this process; in fact it gives it a human presence. For not only does it bring different sounds, smells, colors, and flavors to our streets, it has also altered the composition of many Western towns and countries.

For many in Europe, Muslim immigration is almost synonymous with immigration in general. While the overall numbers of Muslims in western and northern Europe are not huge, in some metropolitan areas Muslims and other immigrants will constitute well over a quarter of the local population during the second decade of the twenty-first century.[8] (It is already

The German capital, Berlin, is known for its large Turkish Muslim population. Here girls perform a traditional Turkish dance in Kreuzberg, a predominantly Turkish neighborhood close to the city center in 2006.

© Atlantide Phototravel/Corbis

estimated that 25 percent of Frankfurt's population is Muslim, and the same goes for Marseille—France's traditional portal to North Africa—and Amsterdam. Paris has a smaller Muslim population, estimated at just below 7.5 percent.)[9] These numbers unsettled many European conventions and made at least one public intellectual eulogize the "Last Days of Europe."[10]

Only very recently did Europeans begin to speak of a "Muslim problem." Until a couple of decades ago, immigrants from Turkey, Pakistan, or Algeria were not lumped together under a single identity. In fact, so diverse are the immigrants' cultures and ethnic backgrounds—even their religious attitudes—that lumping them together requires generalizations and the reconstruction of their identities. But since the 1990s, these diverse ethnic and religious groups have been thrown together, and alarmists in Europe warned against their inability to assimilate. In a short time, western European nations have begun to question their approaches to the issue of integration.

The three most distinct approaches to integration that emerged during the twentieth century are the "multiculturalist" approach associated with the United Kingdom and several northern European countries, the "pillar system" of the Netherlands, and the rigorous assimilation model used in France.

Multiculturalism assumes that people in society act as members of specific communities, all of whom share one civic space. The creation of such spaces draws everyone, the majority and all minorities, into a dialogue about the culture they share.[11] Multiculturalism also assumes that the relationships among the state, the national community, and the individual ought to be mediated by social, religious, and ethnic organizations. Finally, multiculturalism assumes that national identity can be supplemented by other loyalties and identities: the reciprocal relationships between the nation and its minorities should foster social harmony and a sense of personal meaning. As a result, the state grants minorities in Britain a remarkable degree of autonomy and supports their community institutions (the state supports, for example, "faith schools" where the religious traditions of minority groups are upheld). Critics claim that multiculturalism encourages the creation of "parallel societies" that undermine rather than reinforce national solidarity.

The pillar system is often treated as a variation on the multicultural model. Traditionally it divided Dutch society vertically into three groups: Catholics, Protestants, and a "humanist" pillar that included socialists, atheists, and Jews.[12] The communities are meant to run separate and autonomous social and political institutions; thus, similar to the multicultural model, the pillar system promotes distinct "faith-based" schools. Although pillar systems had all but collapsed by the

> *"In the assimilationist model, access to citizenship . . . means that individual cultural backgrounds are erased and overridden by a political community, the nation, that ignores all intermediary communitarian attachments."*
> *– Olivier Roy*

end of the twentieth century, "the ethos, and the legal structure, of separateness persisted, and it was the first and often the most enduring lesson about living in Holland that immigrants learned."[13] During recent decades, the boundaries between the pillars have often been blurred, but when faced with the need to acknowledge a fourth group, namely Muslims, policy makers created a fourth pillar to bring recent immigrants into the political process. Critics of the system argue that the murder of the filmmaker Theo van Gogh in 2004 by an Islamic militant showed that the revised schema

has failed to create a shared, integrated culture in the Netherlands.

The assimilation model calls on immigrants to accept a single national culture. According to scholar Olivier Roy, in the French version (which is often portrayed as the quintessential assimilation model), "access to citizenship . . . means that individual cultural backgrounds are erased and overridden by a political community, the nation, that ignores all intermediary communitarian attachments."[14] Anything local, peculiar to a small group with shared traditions, can be a threat to national cohesion. This is especially true of public displays of that separate identity, such as the wearing of the Islamic veil in public schools. Critics of this model argue that it infringes on minorities' freedom of religious and cultural expression.

These models of integration were amended time and again, so much so that speaking of a French assimilation model can be done only with a great deal of caution and reservation. Interwoven into these integration models were different approaches to naturalization—the process by which an immigrant can become a citizen. Until recently, two "pure" models stood out. The first is based on the legal principle of *jus sanguinis* (Latin for "right of blood"), on which the Germans based their naturalization process. According to this principle, individuals with an ancestor who is or was a German citizen can become citizens too. The German model of their nation (the *Volk*) was that of a people connected by family or blood ties. The second is based on the legal principle of *jus soli* (Latin for "right of soil"), on which the French traditionally based their citizenship. This model allows people born on French soil to become citizens. The

French model of their nation was therefore based on shared geography, experience, and language.

While both citizenship models were adopted across Europe, increased immigration, economic needs, and European Union integration have necessitated many changes, including a law in Germany in 2004 that allows guest workers and their descendants to apply for citizenship. A constant flux in immigration and naturalization laws has rendered it almost impossible to speak of any of these models in their original forms.

France

"The French situation involves many of the issues facing modern democracies in the West: accepting difference, religion in a traditionally secular state, and schools as engines of assimilation."

The French are very proud of their country's willingness to assimilate newcomers. France's streets and outdoor markets burst with both foreign and local smells, music, flavors, and languages. But events such as the 2005 riots in France's poor neighborhoods and the debates surrounding the Islamic veil indicate that all is not well and that an examination of the French integration model could be instructive. We will do so by considering how schoolgirls, children of Muslim immigrants, have challenged official ideas about secularity and the expression of identity. The French situation involves many of the issues facing modern democracies in the West: accepting difference, religion in a traditionally secular state, and schools as engines of assimilation.

Shortly after the end of World War II, European countries turned to colonies and less-developed countries to recruit hundreds of thousands of unskilled laborers from rural areas. These "guest workers" came to aid in the postwar reconstruction efforts, and they were expected to return home when their work was done. But over time it became clear that they were in Europe to stay. By the 1970s, many of these "guests" became immigrants and, in a decade or two, fellow citizens, although not everybody in Europe welcomed these new neighbors. In the 1970s and 1980s, Europe saw the rise of far-right political parties that openly supported anti-immigrant policies. Compounding these problems was an economic crisis—the oil crisis of 1973—that left many immigrants disorganized, unemployed, and competing (with very few job skills) against destitute native-European workers.

In the 1990s, following the end of the Cold War, European societies experienced yet another transformation: the European Union finally moved toward greater integration by creating common economic and political institutions. The process of integrating western Europe (and later Eastern European countries) highlighted Europe's democratic institutions, intellectual legacy, and cultural and scientific achievements. But it also raised concerns about the particular identity of each nation. Many Europeans questioned the value of common governance, currency, and economic organizations, all of which have blurred treasured cultural distinctions. The migration from economically less-developed countries aggravated those fears. In a globalized world, migration introduced new forms of solidarity and identity that extended beyond the borders of the traditional nation-state. Indeed, the Internet, satellite TV, and cell phones provided an instant and live network that connected people of similar cultural backgrounds across the globe.

In France, immigration also threatened national identity from *within*: the immigrants from the former North African colonies of Tunisia, Morocco, and Algeria (known collectively as the Maghreb) struggled to assimilate, and stood out because of their ethnicity, religion, and low social status. Common prejudices led to their broad categorization as "Arabs"—a term that became synonymous with cultural inferiority. Segregation also played a role: these immigrants settled in the suburbs of larger cities, and in the course of a decade or two the traditional European residents of these neighborhoods gradually moved out. It was in these suburbs (*banlieues* in French) that the immigrants began to build cultural and religious institutions. They also developed their own sense of what it meant to be French. Many French wondered whether it was possible to be Algerian and French at the same time, and whether an assertive Muslim minority would fracture France's national unity. These sentiments began to crystallize around the Islamic veil. For many, the veil became symbolic of Muslims' inability to assimilate into mainstream society. Despite protests from girls and women who wore veils insisting that veiling was their personal choice, many Europeans argued that the veil represented Islam's oppression of women, as well as other "illiberal" and "undemocratic" values. Indeed, the veil often came to signify the confrontation of contemporary cultures and the so-called "clash of civilizations."

Generally speaking, the dilemma many European nations face is whether their public spaces and civil society can be reconciled with the expectations of a new religious minority. As religious scholar and philosopher Adam Seligman remarked, "It is not all that clear that the idea of the public arena or public sphere has the same resonance and meanings . . . in other cultures as it does in the West."[15] Some feel that, after centuries of violent struggle, the relationship between state and religion has been settled, so Muslim immigrants need to adapt. By defining religion as a private, personal affair, assimilationists bar it from the civic sphere. In 2008, for example, France's Conseil d'Etat denied citizenship to a 32-year-old Moroccan woman known as Faiza M. because her practice of Islam, including her wearing of the burka, was deemed incompatible with French culture.[16] If you want to become French, say the authorities, you must master the French language and take on French values and culture.

When individuals display religious symbols in public, especially in France, their motives are often seen as a challenge to the status quo. Thus, when the political atmosphere was ripe, the clothing of Muslim immigrants became the subject of myth and misinformation. As people on both sides struggle to preserve their vision of tradition, the conflict has engendered prejudice, discrimination, and fear. While many proponents of secularism

In France's major cities, immigrant communities have been pushed to the fringes. Immigrant families find themselves living in tall, low-cost housing projects, such as this one in Marseille. In these areas, known as *banlieues*, they are often excluded from access to some of the services that those in the city center enjoy.

© David Turnley/CORBIS

expect Muslim immigrants to limit their religious experience to the privacy of their homes and mosques, many devout Muslim women (though by no means all) feel that going anywhere in public without the veil violates their religious rights and sensibilities. While the French proponents of *laïcité** are comfortable with the cathedrals, crosses, and other Christian symbols that adorn their streets, many of them call on the state to stop the public display of Muslim symbols and practices.

But under the surface of this ideological debate many other tensions are roiling. Exclusion and discrimination have isolated the Muslim population since the earliest arrivals; widespread poverty, lack of education, and poor job training made things worse.

Then, between September 2001 and July 2005, there was a series of terrorist attacks across the globe. When airplanes in the United States, trains in Madrid, and subways in London became instruments of militant Islamist mass murder, many became concerned that Islam is incompatible with Western values, and that its legacy is undemocratic and violent. But since Muslim minorities are likely to continue to grow roots in Europe, France—to use the words of anthropologist John Bowen—will have to find a way to reconcile the dilemma of these new and visible differences within it.

---

* *Laïcité,* or *laicism*, is French for "secularity." The term comes from the word *lay* or *laity*, which refers to Christians who did not belong to religious orders or to the clergy.

The First Veil Affair*

"Students' wearing of symbols that indicate their religious beliefs is not in itself incompatible with the principle of laïcité." — The Conseil d'État, 1989

If we try to trace the debate about the veil—better known in France as the "veil affair" (*l'affaire du foulard*)—back to its origins, we find ourselves in the town of Creil in the fall of 1989. At the beginning of the school year, three Muslim girls—the sisters Leila (14 years old) and Fatima (13) Achaboun, of Moroccan parents, and Samira Saidani (15), of Tunisian parents—put on their headscarves and went to Creil's Gabriel-Havez Middle School. The parents of their classmates had come to France from former colonies in the Maghreb: Morocco, Algeria, and Tunisia, where Islam had long been the dominant religion. Though most of the students at the middle school were Muslims, very few chose to wear the veil at school. When the girls refused their principal's demand that they remove their headscarves, they were sent home. After several rounds of negotiations between school administrators, the girls' parents, and local organizations, a compromise was reached: the girls would wear their headscarves in school but drop them down to their shoulders in class.[17] The agreement held for a few days, but when the girls began to cover their heads in class, a new round of negotiations began— this time on a national level. Catholic, Muslim, and Jewish organizations joined the discussion, as did the news media, which linked the story to questions of democracy, secularity, and women's rights. Politicians, political analysts, and public intellectuals tossed their opinions into the mix—the first "veil affair" had been born.

Three girls were suspended from Gabriel-Havez Middle School when they refused to remove their veils.

* Over the last two decades, the use of the French term *foulard*, which means "scarf," was replaced by the term *voile* (French for *veil*). Its use in common French suggests a singular religious motive and style of headscarf. In reality, the reasons vary from piety, to habits, to political protest. The term carries strong religious overtones. It is the common translation of the Arabic term *hijab*.

That year, France celebrated the bicentennial of the French Revolution. On the most celebrated day of the Revolution, July 14, following a military procession, an immense parade passed through Paris. Thousands of performers took part in the parade representing France's diverse population and cultures. Led by France's first socialist president, François Mitterrand, the bicentennial celebrated the revolution that upended the monarchy 200 years earlier. But it was also the celebration of a government that attempted to come to terms with France's ethnic and cultural mix.

Diversity was very much part of the story of Creil. An industrial town north of Paris, Creil was not unlike a thousand other French towns where immigrants from France's former colonies had settled. A tour around these towns revealed, amid your typical French landscape, halal butchers, Moroccan restaurants, bookstores carrying Arabic titles, and many women in headscarves. In marketplaces and on busy streets, the air was filled with a mixture of North African and Western music; the sound of Arabic; and smells, images, and commodities from around the world. Here, within the framework of the French Republic, integration was growing roots.

The news about a fateful event earlier that year began to resonate with many in France. In February 1989, the Iranian leader Ayatollah Khomeini issued a *fatwa** calling for the death of the Indian-born British author, Salman Rushdie. Rushdie's alleged crime? In a novel entitled *The Satanic Verses*, he made comments that were interpreted in Iran as an insult to the prophet Muhammad. The event contributed to the perception of Islam as an intolerant religion, and many French citizens feared that disillusioned Muslim youths would embrace the Ayatollah's antidemocratic religious dogma. Later, in 1995, Algerian Islamists detonated bombs in Lyon and Paris. The public reacted with fear, and many began to regard the veil as a symbol of Islamic radicalization.[18]

Moreover, behind France's embrace of its ethnic groups, social tensions continued to flare up—and not only in political circles. Secondary and high schools became the center of the nation's attention, as assertions of Muslim identity and eruptions of antisemitism became more common. Jews and Arabs—groups largely of North African ancestry—had lived together in the same neighborhoods, walked the same streets, and enjoyed amicable relations for decades. Since the 1990s however, and especially between 2002 and 2004, the two communities grew apart. Their relationship soured.** Reports suggested harassment and violence of Jewish children, especially those who stood out in traditional orthodox clothing (namely, kippas or skullcaps). In some cases, antisemitism was linked to the Arab-Israeli conflict or extremist religious rhetoric. But more fundamental tensions between an assimilated and relatively prosperous community and a poor and demonized community created plenty of anxiety on their own.[19]

In public schools, things got worse. In France's classrooms, teachers reported displays of disrespect and defiance. The teachers brought their grievances to the state. The public schools, however, were

---

* *Fatwa* is a religious decree.
** 70 percent of the 500,000 to 600,000 Jews who live in France come from the same North African countries as French Muslims. But in contrast with most of the Muslim immigrants, Jews have prospered in France. Naturalization became legal in the late eighteenth century, and Jews from Morocco, Tunisia, and Algeria (all the Jews of Algeria were French citizens by law) have consciously assimilated into France's post–World War II society.

chronically short-staffed and lacked funding, resources, and textbooks. Ethnic and economic gaps between teachers and students increased the difficulties of easing the tensions. Critics noted that teachers also lacked the skills necessary to deal with the ethnic and religious tensions in their classrooms. Against this background, the veil became yet another distraction—an issue that divided the student population, raised heated debates inside and outside the Muslim community, and led to occasional outbursts of violence among students. Many critics quickly blamed the crisis on the veil, arguing that the 1989 "veil affair" proved it was "impossible for Muslims to assimilate universal values and/or integrate into French society."[20]

The opposition to the veil quickly transcended traditional party lines. A growing consensus arose: the issue split the country along sectarian or ethnic lines (the French describe this phenomenon with the pejorative term *communautarisme*, which, like the English term sectarianism, implies breaking down society into smaller communities for selfish reasons). And, worse, it violated France's secular tradition. As the Left claimed that Islam might never mesh with human-rights principles, the far Right argued that the Muslim community weakened France's Christian identity. Even traditionally radical groups argued against the veil when feminists attacked the veil as a symbol of male oppression.[21]

The Gabriel-Havez Middle School case was finally referred to France's highest administrative court, the Conseil d'Etat. This court surprised many with its ruling:

> In educational institutions, students' wearing of symbols that indicate their religious beliefs is not in itself incompatible with the principle of "laïcité," to the extent that the wearing of such symbols constitutes the exercise of freedom of expression and freedom to express religious beliefs.[22]

This left the three girls at the heart of the case, Leila Achaboun, Fatima Achaboun, and Samira Saidani, sequestered in their school's library—where they were not permitted to sit in class with the other students. When other schools faced similar dilemmas, teachers sometimes elected to strike, forcing their school's administration to expel veiled Muslim girls. But the Conseil d'Etat repeatedly ruled in favor of girls who insisted on covering their heads.[23]

The Ban on Headscarves in Public Schools

By the early 1990s the tide had turned against the openness of the Mitterrand regime. Anti-immigrant sentiments sent government officials on the offensive against legal and illegal immigrants. As a result, in 1993, the "Pasqua Law" (named after the French interior minister Charles Pasqua) was enacted. The measures included in the law were designed to bring the inflow of migrants to zero. Deemed repressive by many, it impeded, and even criminalized, several traditional forms of immigration, and made it harder for French-born sons and daughters

© AP Photo/Francois Mori

A French police car is parked outside the Paris mosque immediately after the 9/11 attacks. The mosque was founded in 1926, a gift from the French government in recognition of the sacrifices of Muslim colonial soldiers during World War I.

of immigrants to become citizens (a right that was traditionally extended automatically to anybody born on French soil). Other measures—random identity checks, for example—were seen as specifically targeting North Africans' civil rights.[24] In 1994, after additional clashes between school administrators and Muslim girls, the minister of education, François Bayrou, decreed that "ostentatious" signs of religious affiliation would be prohibited in all schools.[25] In what the media called the "Bayrou Memo," Bayrou called for a law banning headscarves in schools, declaring:

In France the national and republican projects have been identified with a certain idea of citizenship. This French idea of the nation and republic by nature respects all convictions, particularly religious and political beliefs and cultural traditions. But it rules out the breaking down of the nation into separate communities which are indif-ferent to one another. . . . The nation is not only a group of citizens who hold individual rights. It is a community with a [common] destiny.[26]

While the "Bayrou Memo" did not send scores of Muslim girls home, its language had a long-term effect on the debate.

After the attacks on the World Trade Center and the Pentagon on September 11, 2001, people began to speak of a "clash of civilizations" between the West and the Muslim world. This fit neatly with the xenophobic rhetoric being used by France's National Front, the right-wing party led by Jean-Marie Le Pen, and the party did better than ever in the 2002 elections.

The effects of 9/11 on the Muslim population in France were manifold. Newspapers carried reports of an increase in hate crimes against Islamic establishments and in the numbers of Muslims who were attacked on the streets; public speeches attacking the rights of immigrants were cheered, and many North African immigrants reported a growing resentment to their presence in France.[27] A Moroccan immigrant described the situation with a joke: "When Samia wants to rent a studio apartment that has been advertised in Paris, she finds upon giving her name that the apartment has been unavailable since September 11."[28] Called "Arabs" until that date, now immigrants from North Africa were part of a "Muslim problem."

When a series of new veil stories appeared in the news, it seemed quite obvious to the public that something had to be done. Many teachers and administrators demanded that the government step in and order Muslim schoolgirls to remove their headscarves to protect the secularity of public schools. And that is what happened. A few people argued that the veil was a legitimate form of cultural and religious expression; others questioned the thinking of those who would expel from school the veiled girls they portrayed as victims of Islamic oppression.[29] Some in the Muslim population saw racism at work in the new policy. A 31-year-old Moroccan protested:

I find that it's really an attitude on the part of teachers that is really racist, truly. That, for me, is a racist act. We cannot exclude girls because they wear the headscarf. . . . It's really pointing a finger at them, and then vis-à-vis the culture of the child, they say to her "your culture, it's not good." You don't have a right to judge like that.[30]

To some, the best approach involved respect: "The problem could be resolved by respecting the freedom of expression and the freedom to express oneself in all the domains, especially if this liberty does not harm others."[31]

But in a world enormously affected by the terrorist attacks of 9/11, the mood in France has decidedly shifted against the veil. On April 19, 2003, France's minister of the interior, Nicolas Sarkozy, initiated a new campaign to draw Muslim immigrants into mainstream French society. For more than 10 years, the fissures between France's Catholic majority and its Muslim minority had engendered endless grumbling, shouting, and more or less ineffective efforts at harmony and integration. Sarkozy, with the 2007 presidential election in mind, made immigration a central theme of his "law and order" campaign. At a gathering of the Union of France's Islamic Organizations, Sarkozy went straight to the heart of the matter:

In France we cannot have an Islam which speaks against Republican values. . . . The law says that the photograph on a national identity card must be taken bareheaded, whether the holder is a man or a woman. This obligation is respected by Catholic nuns, and by all the women who live in France. Nothing would justify a different law for women of the Muslim faith.[32]

Booed by the crowd, Sarkozy was cheered by politicians, religious groups, intellectuals, and teachers who clamored against the headscarf.[33] From identity photos the focus soon returned to schools, where growing ethnic tensions were often blamed on this item of clothing. After a radio speech in which Prime Minister Jean-Pierre Raffarin stated that Muslim headscarves should "absolutely" be prohibited in public schools, a new law seemed inevitable. A string of endorsements followed, prompting President Jacques Chirac to appoint a

Alma Lévy, (left) with her sister Lila, in October 2003. Although their Jewish father did not approve of their decision to don headscarves, he sought to defend their right to attend school by criticizing the rationale for their expulsion.

commission to study religion and secularity in France and prepare recommendations.[34] Although the commission's brief said nothing about it, no one doubted that the headscarf was the central issue.

"Splitting society into communities [communautarisme] cannot be the choice for France." – President Jacques Chirac, 2003

In this charged atmosphere, a new headscarf affair exploded in the French media. Attention was now directed to Aubervilliers, a densely populated suburb northeast of Paris, with a large immigrant community. In September 2003, Alma Lévy, 16 years old, and her sister Lila Lévy, 18 years old, showed up to school wearing veils that covered a large part of their faces (they wore what was commonly referred to as "Muslim" headscarves or *foulards islamiques* in French). When asked to remove their veils, they refused. Again, the argument was that their veils violated France's secularity. The defiant sisters were daughters of Laurent Lévy, a

Jewish atheist who worked for an antiracist organization (Mouvement contre le Racisme et pour l'Amitié entre les Peuples), and a Kabyle mother from Algeria who never wore the veil. The separated couple did not approve of their daughters' actions; the father in fact encouraged them to give it up. Eventually, the girls' refusal to replace their "Muslim" headscarves with an acceptable light scarf led to their expulsion from school. Moreover, Alma's and Lila's Jewish last name puzzled many French and exacerbated fears about racial mixing and conversion to Islam.[35]

In the meantime, the commission finished its work. In December 2003 it released its report, "*Laïcité* and the Republic," and made several recommendations—including measures to promote the recognition of France's religious and ethnic diversity. Chirac acted on one proposal alone: the banning of visible religious symbols in schools.

Soon after the report had been made public, Chirac gave a speech about the French model of integration, which stresses the acquisition of the French language and other mainstream cultural habits. He declared that the French principle of laïcité was "not negotiable":

> One thing is certain: the answer to these concerns does not lie in the . . . withdrawal into oneself or one's community. On the contrary, it lies in the affirmation of our wish to live together, bolstering the common fervor, in remaining true to our history and our values.[36]

"Splitting society into communities [communautarisme] cannot be the choice for France," Chirac declared. "School is a republican sanctuary." Therefore, to protect students from the "divisive ill winds, which drive people apart and set them against one another . . . [,] the wearing of clothes or signs which conspicuously denote a religious affiliation must be prohibited at school."[37]

Since the turn of the 1990s, scholar Joan Wallach Scott explains, the veil has come to symbolize the differences between the European French and the Muslim minority.[38] But why was so much fuss made over an item of clothing? Why did people begin to view it as infringing on the principle of secularity and other French values? And how did it threaten a national identity?

A young Muslim girl protests the French government over its proposed headscarf bans in Paris, 2003. Her sign reads "Discrimination: action of isolating, making an unjust distinction in the treatment of different categories of people."

© Frederick Florin/AFP/Getty Images

Secularism in France

"We must refuse everything to the Jew as a nation and accord everything to the Jew as an individual." – Clermont-Tonnerre, 1789

In 1789, the common people of France rose up against the crown, the hereditary nobility, and the Church. These institutions were not permanently extinguished, and the French state struggled for another century to separate itself from the Church. According to scholars Jonathan Laurence and Justin Vaisse, by the late nineteenth century the government functioned as a progressive and democratic force: "In the hope of weakening organized religion's potentially seditious effects," they wrote, the state attempted "to relegate religion strictly to the private sphere and regulate its entry into the public sphere."[39]

During the Revolution, the French agreed to grant the Jews who lived in France full civil rights and citizenship (the term used for this process was called "emancipation"). But the way civil rights were given to the Jews was very telling. In 1789, a deputy of the revolutionary National Constituent Assembly named Clermont-Tonnerre (1757–1792) put it succinctly: "We must refuse everything to the Jew as a nation and accord everything to the Jew as an individual."[40] The Jews accepted this model; by and large, they assimilated into French culture and adopted its national identity. They kept their religion private. This formula served France as it integrated religious and ethnic minorities for the next two centuries. The state granted them full rights as individual citizens but refused to involve itself with their group aspirations.

This consolidation of a secular, independent state goes back to that time as well. During the nineteenth century, policymakers in France were faced with the challenges of nation building. For centuries, the area where France is today was divided into several regions that had their own languages and customs. Against this background, the divisive role that the Catholic Church often played was deemed especially harmful. The state and the French secular parties objected to the Church's power and influence in French society—especially to its Jesuit schools, where the ideals of the French Republic were shunned. In 1905, after years of conflict and negotiations, the separation of church and state became law. Although the 1905 law was modified many times, it is still regarded as the legal foundation of French secularism (*laïcité*). At its core is the belief that religion is a private matter and that it has no role to play in the public life of France.

In order to strengthen France's secular identity, republican policy makers emphasized the creation of a common culture rooted in its national history, literature, and culture, as well as in a uniform French language. The process of nation-building therefore included the creation of not only a national economic infrastructure, but also the marginalization of regional differences and the establishment of a national, secular education system. Indeed, education was to take center stage in this process: it was to be the great homogenizer of the French nation.

Secularity in the French Public Schools

"In Europe, church and state are still intertwined in ways that secular Christians hardly notice but which nonetheless penalize religious minorities." — Jytte Klausen

Towards the end of the century, in the 1880s, a minister of education named Jules Ferry took on the project of creating a modern, secular education system. As scholar Joan Wallach Scott observed, he oversaw the creation of a body of laws that "made primary education compulsory for boys and girls and . . . effectively banished from the classroom religion as a subject and priests and nuns as teachers."[41] A contemporary *New York Times* journalist reported, the "government was accused of striking a blow at religion."[42] For Ferry viewed the school as

> . . . the agent of assimilation; the goal of its pedagogy was to instill a common republican political identity in children from a diversity of backgrounds. The school was to effect a transition from private to public, from the world of the locality and the family to that of the nation. Teachers were the crucial element in this process—secular missionaries, charged with converting their pupils to the wonders of science and reason. . . . A shared language, culture, and ideological formation—and so a nation one and indivisible—was to be the outcome of the educational process.[43]

The success of the Ferry laws of 1881 and 1882 was impressive: they helped launch France into the next century as a centralized, industrial nation and unified its citizens to the point that most of the vernaculars used before the reform are now virtually extinct. In the minds of many in France, education became the most important vehicle for assimilation.

Ferry's educational campaign had an additional, related aspect: France's "civilizing mission" (*mission civilisatrice*), of which

This caricature of Jules Ferry was featured in the French newspaper "Men of Today" in 1880. Shown with a bellows under his arm, Ferry viewed public schools as academies where the secular state's values were to be instilled.

he was a passionate supporter. Ferry, who rose to prominence in the 1880s, served as minister of education, minister of foreign affairs, and finally prime minister. During those decades, when France was expanding it colonial holdings, Ferry also assumed the role of an ideologue for the French empire and argued that "the superior races have a right because they have a duty. They have the duty to civilize the inferior races." France, he emphasized, should not just rule over people he saw as "backward." Instead, it was its mission to educate them about Western values, culture, and intellectual achievements. Indeed, France left a legacy of industry, technology, and culture when it retreated from its colonies in the middle of the twentieth century. But the civilizing mission hardened the feelings of the colonial subjects. Many of them found Ferry's approach arrogant and thought that, in fact, it may have been a pretext—France simply wanted to assert its superiority and exploit them.[46]

The hard feelings about France's "civilizing mission" carried over into its public schools, where France, in fact, applied it both to its own citizens and to newcomers. Fifty years after France left its colonies, the model of assimilation through education failed many of the immigrants. Many of them, especially those who came from less-developed countries, felt that the French public school system contributed to a growing distance between the promises of the French Republic and the ordinary lives of young people from immigrant backgrounds. Nevertheless, Ferry's ideal of republican education has not lost its currency and his insistence that religion exit the classroom has only gained adherents. Education Minister Bayrou's 1994 memo argued that the ideal of French republicanism is constructed firstly at school.

School is the space which more than any other involves education and integration where all children and all youth are to be found, learning to live together and respect one another. If in this school there are signs of behavior which show that they cannot conform to the same obligations, or attend the same courses and follow the same programs, it negates this mission.[47]

During the height of the headscarf debate, it was clear what "behavior" the minister referred to.

To achieve uniformity across the board, schools are centrally administered by the government. It determines the curriculum, chooses textbooks, hires and trains teachers, and dispenses money and resources. So uniform is the system that on any given day, according to an old joke, every French sixth-grader has her textbook open to the same page. The problem with such homogeneity, according to education expert Leslie Limage, is that "there is little acknowledgement of the cultural and linguistic diversity which make up the school population and of France and French society in general."[48]

Efforts have been made to acknowledge the diversity of students in schools, including revising textbooks to include the history of immigration to France, and the Ministry of Education has recently encouraged teachers to discuss with their students the ethnic and religious variety they see around them. In fact, as early as 1982, affirmative action (or "positive discrimination") and the creation of zones where the state has made provisions of additional resources and funding ("educational priority zones") have attempted to shift power away from the center, giving local authorities many more resources to work with.[49]

Still, most teachers are asked to follow a common national curriculum and are often discouraged from raising the issue of ethnic identities.[50] When researchers looked at the modern French educational system, they found a deep-seated suspicion of "multiculturalism" and reported that the vast majority of "the literature used by [French] teachers was by French writers of European descent, reflecting France's literary tradition as outlined in the canon."[51] Many citizens of North African descent, whose parents and grandparents lived under French colonial rule, find that this focus leaves little room to address the injustice their families endured under French colonialism.* Moreover, French teachers face many challenges for which they are not prepared: the frustration of kids from poor suburban ghettos, rowdy classrooms, children from broken families, crime, language barriers, and a shortage of funds and other resources.

Regulating religion—which for France has historically meant Catholicism—has not banished it. Indeed, claims regarding France's secularity tend to ignore many cultural norms and institutions whose origins can be traced to the Catholic Church. In fact, throughout Europe, Christianity remains very powerful vis-à-vis other religions. Danish-American political scientist Jytte Klausen explains: "In Europe, church and state are still intertwined in ways that secular Christians hardly notice but which nonetheless penalize religious minorities." In public areas, the Catholic legacy is highly visible in the cathedrals, churches, and public buildings in every city, town, and village, and the French national holidays continue to reflect the Church calendar.

But although 85 percent of France's population is more or less associated with the Catholic Church, the majority of them do not attend church on a regular basis. For many, their religious affiliation provides a cultural framework, which includes holidays, vocabulary, and vaguely defines values associated with Catholicism. But the vast majority of the French see themselves as secular.

That said, while the French can take advantage of numerous Catholic schools, and many Jewish ones, only a reluctant effort has been made to support Muslim schools.

Tourists line the pedestrian *Pont des Arts* for a nighttime view of Notre Dame Cathedral in Paris. The iconic Notre Dame is one of the oldest religious buildings in Paris.

© Fernand Ivaldi/Getty Images

* A positive view of French colonialism continues to be promoted by some officials. In 2005, when a law was passed calling for the recognition of the tens of thousands of North African soldiers who fought side by side with the French in War World II (known as *harikis*), it also mandated universities to develop programs emphasizing the positive role France played in its colonies, especially in North Africa. The law is no longer in effect as of 2008.

Mixed Origin: Religious Groups in Contemporary France

A century or so after France colonized northern and western Africa, factories drew unskilled laborers from Algeria, Morocco, and Tunisia. With the exception of schooling, the government did little to integrate these new arrivals, most of them Muslims, into mainstream society, assuming that after the labor shortage among native Frenchmen ended that these "guest workers" would return to their native countries.[53] When the public realized that these newcomers—often simply and crassly referred to as "Arabs"—would never leave, many demanded that they find ways to fit into French society—just as immigrants had done for many years before them. While, traditionally, the Left (people associated with the socialist and communist parties in France) embraced the cause of fair treatment of the North African workers, others objected to their presence in France. To them, a large body of foreign immigrants undermined France's national identity.

Charles de Gaulle, president of France for a decade after leading the Free French forces during World War II, outlined his views on national identity in 1959, during the Algerian War of Independence (1954–1962). In a conversation with his close friend and confidant Alain Peyrefitte, de Gaulle described his feelings on a multiethnic France. His language was blunt:

It is very good that there are yellow Frenchmen, black Frenchmen, brown Frenchmen. They prove that France is open to all races and that she has a universal mission. But on the condition they remain a small minority. Otherwise, France would no longer be France. We are after all before all else a European people of the white race, our culture Greek and Latin, our religion Christian. . . . Try to mix oil and vinegar. Shake the bottle. After a bit, they will separate again. Arabs are Arabs, French are French. Do you believe that the French nation can absorb ten million Muslims, who tomorrow will be twenty million and the day after forty? If we were to adopt integration, if all the Arabs and Berbers of Algeria were considered French, what would prevent them from coming to settle in the big cities where the standard of living is so much higher? My village would no longer be called Colombey-les-Deux-Eglises [Colombey of Two Churches]—it would be Colombey-les-Deux-Mosquées [Colombey of Two Mosques].[54]

Some of the prejudices against Arabs expressed in de Gaulle's speech can be traced to Jules Ferry's time, when France sought to "civilize" the "backward," or uneducated, natives it encountered across the world. Other prejudices have to do with the notion of ethnic purity, which conflicts with the fact that France is (and has been for decades) a home to many minorities.

While de Gaulle's vision did not materialize, some five million Muslims do live in France today, the majority of them of North African descent, out of a total population of 61 million.[55] Roughly half of them are French citizens, but their growing presence in France—a presence sometimes highlighted by a darker skin color and, in some cases, Arab or Muslim traditional dress—has shaken the national

French President Charles de Gaulle greets supporters in Lille in 1966. De Gaulle was a French hero during World War II. Prior to the allied landings in Normandy he coordinated the French Resistance, or underground freedom fighters, from exile and then led French armies in the field after those landings. After the war he became a key social and political figure, serving as president during the Algerian War of Independence.

ideal de Gaulle laid out. France has also experienced a European migration, which kept feeding a diverse population in the French "melting pot."[56] And most historians agree that it took centuries and tremendous investments to turn France's peasants, who shared neither traditions nor language, into a nation with a shared identity. Historian Eugen Weber argued that, in fact, a unified national identity did not emerge in France until after World War I.[57]

Indeed, France is and has always been made up of a collection of different cultural and religious groups. Some of them fared better than others. The Jews, a small but noticeable group since the first century CE, were "emancipated" at the time of the French Revolution, gaining the rights of full citizens. Among those who emigrated from Africa in the nineteenth and twentieth centuries were Algerian Jews, who were formally offered citizenship in 1870. Despite being a traditional target for racial attacks, Jews slowly integrated into French society. While there were signs of progress, there were also reminders that Jews were seen by some as different, disloyal, and not to be trusted. Maybe no story better represents the precarious position of French Jews in the nineteenth century—and, by extension, other minorities—than the Dreyfus affair.

In 1894, Alfred Dreyfus, a Jewish French officer, was arrested and accused of selling military secrets to the Germans. The false accusations and public debates surrounding his trial drew attention to deep-seated antisemitism in France. The affair split the French republic. Leading artists and intellectuals split into camps, some supporting Dreyfus, some supporting his accusers. In 1906, after 12 years and massive public protests, Dreyfus was exonerated and restored to his military post.

In the first decades of the twentieth century, cosmopolitan Paris became home to immigrants and refugees looking to create a new life for themselves. Among them were Jews. The freedom of those years was first strained by the global depression of the 1930s and then later by the Nazi occupation. Contrary to the republican spirit, the Vichy government collaborated with Nazi antisemitic policies. While many French are justly proud of the Resistance and of those who risked their lives to rescue Jews, Jews suffered under the occupation. Jews were prohibited from working, forced to wear yellow stars identifying them as "other," property was confiscated, and families were separated. Jews were confined to concentration camps (some German Jewish refugees were sent first to camps as Germans and then a second time as Jews).

In the end, 75,000 Jews were deported from France to Nazi concentration camps where tens of thousands of them were murdered.

"First-generation immigrants had been trying all their lives to take up as little space and make as little noise as possible . . . and no one was troubled by lives whose main object was to be as light and elusive as the wind."
— *Tahar Ben Jelloun*

Following the Holocaust—or what is commonly known as the *shoah* in France—the government vowed that the horrors of the war years would never be repeated. The Holocaust served as a reminder that sectarian ideas or anything that might be seen as splitting the country on racial or religious grounds should be condemned. Many Jews felt that the best way to integrate was not to stand out. Other immigrants seemed to accept that stance as well. Some French families had comefrom nearby European countries such as Italy, Spain, and Portugal. They had settled quickly in France and within a generation many had become citizens, attained linguistic skills, and assimilated into the national culture. They were mostly white

and Christian—their presence neither stirred deep resentment nor led to an identity crisis.

But immigrants who came to France after World War II did not have the same experience. (See the map in the reading *Integration and Exclusion*.) Several waves of immigrants made the relatively short trip across the Mediterranean to France from the Maghreb. Unskilled single men from the remote rural regions of these poor countries were recruited as "guest workers" in the post-war reconstruction efforts; poorly paid, they were exposed to extreme conditions, including searing heat, choking dust, and toxic dyes and gases.[58]

Both the "guest workers" and the French at first assumed that these men would return to their countries of origin. Often illiterate, they spoke little or no French and remained attached to their native customs and traditions. They were settled in overcrowded, temporary shelters on the peripheries of industrial centers, "mud cities comprising makeshift homes without electricity or plumbing, little different from Third World shantytowns."[59] Those who decided to stay risked deportation: as workers without proper papers, they aimed to attract as little attention as possible while getting by.

France, in need of immigrant labor to help rebuild the country after WWII, established precarious housing slums for Maghrebian immigrants at the start of the 1950s.

French Ethnic Population Chart

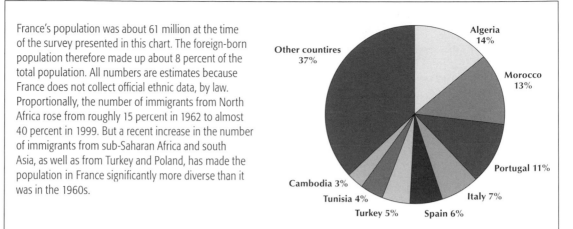

France's population was about 61 million at the time of the survey presented in this chart. The foreign-born population therefore made up about 8 percent of the total population. All numbers are estimates because France does not collect official ethnic data, by law. Proportionally, the number of immigrants from North Africa rose from roughly 15 percent in 1962 to almost 40 percent in 1999. But a recent increase in the number of immigrants from sub-Saharan Africa and south Asia, as well as from Turkey and Poland, has made the population in France significantly more diverse than it was in the 1960s.

Other countires 37%
Algeria 14%
Morocco 13%
Portugal 11%
Italy 7%
Spain 6%
Turkey 5%
Tunisia 4%
Cambodia 3%

Source: The Organization for Economic Cooperation and Development, 2005.[63]

In a very personal study of racism in his adopted country, French-Moroccan novelist Tahar Ben Jelloun wrote that first-generation immigrants (like many other immigrants around the world) had "been trying all their lives to take up as little space and make as little noise as possible, to pass unnoticed. . . . They melted into the landscape, and no one was troubled by lives whose main object was to be as light and elusive as the wind."[60] Most never expected much help from the nation that had previously colonized and exploited their home countries. The Algerians, who arrived in the 1950s, Ben Jelloun recalled, lived "in a no-man's-land, a place where exclusion was automatic, unreflecting, taken for granted. They thought they were living in peace, a small kind of peace made up of work, sleep, and brief Sunday respites, together with the trivia of everyday life."[61]

A significant number of this generation have become successful in France and developed a lifestyle not unlike other Frenchmen. They moved into private homes in Marseille and Paris and joined the ranks of the middle class. But they are the exception: the majority of this disadvantaged population has not managed to keep up with other immigrant groups in education and income.[62]

One reason was unemployment. In 1973, following the international oil crisis, the post–World War II economic boom imploded. Never fully integrated into France's powerful trade unions, unskilled immigrant workers were the first to lose their jobs. Those fortunate enough to keep their jobs faced the bitter resentment of unemployed French citizens. Anti-Arab sentiments boosted right-wing political parties, whose leaders spoke for the first time of an "immigration problem."

Over the years, the French government attempted to address the difficulties facing these immigrants, who lived under appalling conditions. Since the late 1960s, several generations of housing projects have been built on the outskirts of Paris, Marseille, Lyon, and other big cities to accommodate the immigrants.[64] But these government-subsidized refuges created a new problem: they created enclaves (or ghettos, as the French would call them), which contributed to the isolation of the immigrants and their sons and daughters.

© David Turnley/CORBIS

The majority of immigrants who came to work in France were relocated by the government to isolated high-rise housing projects on the outskirts of France's larger cities.

As the French economy has shifted from industry to services, professional occupations, and e-commerce, the children of North African immigrants have found themselves locked in these neighborhoods with very few exit options.

Socially, culturally, geographically, and economically isolated, immigrants and their children attempted to create a small replica of the homeland.[65] In the 1980s, a new generation of French with North African ancestry came of age. They began to talk about these enclaves as a new a zone of engagement. Singer Karim Kacel, the son of Algerian immigrants, was among the first to do so. In a famous song released in 1984 called "Banlieue," he described a 17-year-old who, suffocated by the grip of poverty and exclusion, dreams of fleeing the suburbs of Paris.[66]

Kacel and others evoked images of shattered hope—the disillusionment with the hope for a better life shared by immigrants around the globe. In the 1980s, this generation came of age. Youths "from every suburb," in the words of Ben Jelloun, found the courage to "invent a new and original identity for themselves, owing nothing to their parents and making no gesture toward French society. They no longer feel confused, at least for the moment."[67] Soon these North African French youth would demand recognition and fair treatment—and, in doing so, would shift the focus of France's debate on the issue of ethnic and religious identity.[68] Indeed, in the 1980s, the bonds that held the old social camps and pitted the working class against the middle classes had loosened up and lost some allure. Instead, many young French began to identify themselves by their ethnicity or religion, and French of North African origin (though by no means just this group) embarked on a search for alternatives to the official national narrative. When they eventually rejected France's official history, they were looking to affirm their identity, to condemn the injustice done to their community, and to claim an equal voice in France's democratic process.

The Beur Generation

"For the vast majority of 'second-generation' French Muslims, the search for identity is represented in the veil and the study of Islam, but, indeed, some of them go on to protest the treatment of Muslims in France."

When fifteen teenagers set out on foot from the southern city of Marseille in October 1983, they hoped their march might draw attention to anti-Arab violence and intolerance. They invented a new name for themselves—Beurs, which was a play on the term *Arabes* (Arabs)*—in an attempt to escape the negative connotation associated with being Arab. The "March of the Beurs" climaxed in Paris two months later, as a crowd estimated at 100,000 welcomed this new generation of civil rights activists inspired by the likes of Mohandas Gandhi and Martin Luther King, Jr.[69]

The Beurs grew up in the empty spaces that surround Paris and other big cities. "Relegated to the periphery, in exile everywhere, nomads in their own existence, they go round in circles," reflected author Ben Jelloun in the 1980s. He saw them as lost: "Even if they have French identity cards, they are not sure . . . where they belong." They needed, he argued, to acquire a proper cultural identity, something that would "attest both to their identity and their difference, thus giving them a face and a voice."[70] Neither the French identity nor the Maghrebian seemed right, particularly to young people for whom a traditional collective identity associated with either France or the Maghreb had far

less appeal than an identity without a specific location.

For many, religion helps to affirm identity, serving as a bulwark against social discrimination and rejection. The turn toward Islam makes sense to Dutch political scientist Frank Buijs, who sees it as a form of self-expression little different from the youthful fashion statements so common among American adolescents.[71] This trend also marks a change in the political discourse in Europe. In the earlier parts of the twentieth century, political debates focused on social groups and the tensions between them (the working class versus the middle class, for example). Since the 1980s, debates about ethnic and religious identity came to the fore, despite resis-tance from both Left and Right politicians who clung to the idea of one universal French identity. For the vast majority of second-generation French Muslims, the search for individual identity is represented in the veil and the study of Islam. Indeed, some of them go on to protest the treatment of Muslims in France. Girls often turn to the veil to experiment with their new identity. Boys sometimes turn to local preachers to study Arabic and learn the Quran. A small number of Beurs even seek the advice of militant imams who preach hate

---

* *Beur* is a specimen of French slang called *Verlan*—the inversion of sounds and syllables in a word to create a new word. The word *Verlan* was created by inverting the two syllables in the word *envers*, which means "backwards." The word *Beurs* implies something more positive than *Arabes*, a term that's often used to malign immigrant groups.

The name "Beurger King Muslim" is a play on the slang word *Beur*, used for North Africans. This is a fast food place serving only Halal meat in Clichy-sous-Bois.

© Owen Franken/Corbis.

and destruction, a trend that has raised concerns in the French public that the Islamic revival among the disillusioned youth of the *banlieues*—and the veil in particular—will lead to radicalism and terror.*

Since the late 1990s, many have dwelt on the religious and ethnic divisions in French society. An alternative view is that of Jonathan Laurence and Justin Vaisse, who argue that these apparent divisions are constantly being bridged as French men and women from European backgrounds dip into the food markets, the music, the art and literature of their North African neighbors. In sports, for example, fans embrace soccer players of North African origin as readily as today's white fans in the United States celebrate African American athletes.[72] The most beloved player on the French national team, Zinedine Zidane (who led France to a World Cup championship in 1998 and to the World Cup final in 2006), grew up among the disenfranchised youths of North African descent in Le Castellane—an immigrant neighborhood in Marseille. Zidane explained his dual identity:

[F]or me, the most important thing is that I still know who I am. Every day I think about where I come from and I am still proud to be who I am: first, a Kabyle [a non-Arab Algerian] from Le Castellane, then an Algerian from Marseille, and then a Frenchman.[73]

Clearly, some in France feel that there is room for Frenchmen who rank their minority identities together with their national identities.

The popular music created by young Muslim artists has also caught the imagination of many young French people, who view it as authentic, rebellious, and cool; critics regard it as a stylistic breakthrough. Combining the rhythmic feel of American hip-hop and rap with North African tunes and instruments, musicians from the *banlieues* have created a unique new sound. Scholar Valérie Orlando recently wrote, "Hip-hop culture and rap music have become the most popular means through which [immigrants] voice their demands for cultural and ethnic recognition."[74] This music also expresses the main con-

---

* In the past, the *banlieues* were viewed as dreamlike neighborhoods of the middle and upper classes around Paris and other urban centers. But since the 1990s, Jonathan Laurence and Justin Vaisse have noted, "the *banlieue* [became] rather like a ghetto phenomenon. . . . These neighborhoods are marked by poverty, welfare dependence, black markets, broken families, and single mothers. . . . In these neighborhoods one finds a mix of everyday violence, gang-type social systems, an indigenous code of conduct and honor, the assertion of 'masculine' identity, and an emphasis on territoriality" (Laurence and Vaisse, *Integrating Islam*, 36).

Zinedine Zidane plays for France during a friendly soccer match against Algeria in 2001. Zidane was raised in a *banlieue* outside of Marseille and is of Algerian descent. Thanks to his soccer skills and background, he is a national icon and hero to many in the country.

cerns of the third-generation Beurs: "French rappers," writes André J. M. Prévos, "express opposition to the social order, and to political and economic systems which have led to what they call the 'oppression' of minorities (Arab immigrants in particular). French rappers tell about the hardships of everyday life in the poorer suburbs, which they often characterize as *le ghetto*."[75]

The hybrid origins of French rap, its halting beats and blunt lyrics, speak of a new, assertive generation of Beurs forging their identity at the crossroads of a globalized world. Like veiling, this music often suggests the search for a voice and a place in society; many also use these expressive

"Hip-hop culture and rap music have become the most popular means through which [immigrants] voice their demands for cultural and ethnic recognition." – Valérie Orlando

means to defy the boundaries and restrictions that mainstream society imposes on the excluded. These young people are inventing a new culture that is basically transatlantic; although Beurs could hardly shed their ethnic and religious

heritage, their music smacks largely of youthful rebellion and Western consumer culture. Islam is just one of many factors interwoven into the complex fabric of self-definition that these young Beurs are constantly weaving.

If a 13-year-old girl covers her head with a scarf, she joins a community of devout Muslims across the world, but does this mean she is rejecting all of her connections to her country? No: the majority of second- and third-generation Muslims express a deep connection to France. Their main complaint is a feeling of being exiles in their own country, left out of the society they long to join. One can hear some of this in Raï, popular music sung in French and Arabic that originated among Algerian Bedouins. In a song called "I Don't Think It's Going to Be Possible" (*"Je crois que ça va pas être possible"*), a group called Zebda* expresses its frustration with a society that offers endless goods and services to everyone but them. In this and many other songs, one hears the pain of failed assimilation, the desire for full membership in French society. Too often, writes journalist Stéphanie Giry, the heated discussion of recent decades "obscures a critical fact: that the vast majority of Europe's 15–20 million

---

* The name of the band is important: *zebda* means "butter" in Arabic (and Hebrew), a play on the term *Beur,* which, when spelled *beurre*, means "butter" in French.

Muslims have nothing to do with radical Islamism and are struggling hard to fit in, not opt out."[76]

This is supported by a Pew study released in July 2006. The research found that Muslims in Europe "worry about their future, but their concern is more economic than religious or cultural." Moreover, "Muslims there do not generally believe that most Europeans are hostile toward people of their faith." The same report found little evidence of a major backlash against Muslims in France and other European countries in the wake of the attacks in New York and London; the French public believed that French Muslims "want to adopt French customs—a view held by an overwhelming majority of Muslims in France."[77] In France, Muslims marry non-Muslims more often than in any other European country, a hint that assimilation is taking place at the most intimate level.[78] The idea of a "clash of civilizations" carries little weight with European Muslims, whose everyday conflicts with the traditional majority have nothing to do with jihad or a crusade. The Pew researchers found that Muslims across Europe have faith in democracy, and this is especially true in France.[79]

Research shows that Muslim girls fare better in schools than their fellow male students. Consider Fatima, whose experience as a student in the 1990s was recorded by scholar Trica Keaton. One of a growing number of well-integrated French Muslim girls, Fatima performed brilliantly in school, a crucial first step toward professional success in France's remarkably regimented society. Raised in a traditional family by a strict father (who would not allow his daughters, for religious reasons, to go out at night or join in after-school events), she described her background as "an advantage and an asset" rather than a burden. "I am Muslim," she wrote in her journal. "I don't practice, really, but I observe Ramadan . . . I don't eat pork; I don't drink alcohol." At the same time, she continued, "I find myself totally integrated in France, so I feel at home everywhere. . . . My identity is: French of Algerian origin, of Muslim religion."[80]

Fatima's story belongs to a larger, international epic, a twentieth- and twenty-first century wave of hybrid identities. Her experience—and that of Zidane and many others—suggests the many possible shades of French identity in a globalized world that is both expanding and shrinking.

In the years that followed the 2003 headscarf ban, many of the girls who refused to take off their veils in public schools have settled into progressive Catholic schools where they are allowed to wear the hijab, much like the teachers who are allowed to wear the habit. The Muslim population as a whole came to accept the ban issued by the state in 2004, although Muslims around the world initially attacked it.[*] Thousands of French Muslims, including prominent leaders, did originally protest the law as an attack on their religion. But within a year the public debate subsided. Journalist Adam Sage summarized its effect:

In the year since the law was implemented 626 girls have arrived for

---

[*] In one extreme example, the so-called Islamic Army in Iraq kidnapped two French journalists, threatening murder if the ban was not repealed. The kidnapping took France by surprise, as well as the Muslim leadership in France. According to *Al-Ahram Weekly*, an Egyptian newspaper, French Muslims "have been sparing no effort to demonstrate their full condemnation of this kidnapping and their opposition to attempts to retract veil related laws through violence or the threat of violence. The strong presence of veiled women and bearded men was an unmistakable sign that devout Muslims are equally horrified by what has happened." See Dina Ezzat, "Not in Our Name," *Al-Ahram Weekly* online, 2–8 September 2004, *http://weekly.ahram.org.eg/2004/706/re7.htm* (accessed November 16, 2007).

French students protest education cutbacks in 2008. Social protests in France have typically been closely associated with students. Here, students from across cultures demonstrate together.

lessons wearing a Muslim headscarf—compared with 1,465 over the previous 12 months and more than 5,000 at the start of the decade. Of these, 496 agreed to remove them when summoned for a talk with the head teacher. A further 45 refused and were expelled.[81]

But this step toward the secular French ideal does not appear to have reduced the poverty, tensions, and violence in the *banlieues*. The flames and destruction periodically emanating from these poor and largely segregated neighborhoods suggest that the French republican secularism/assimilation model is in crisis. In fact, the continued economic despair of many minorities in France has often strengthened the bond of religious communities, which rally together as a means of empowerment in the face

> **"Although most experts agree that the [2005 Paris] riots centered around socio-economic problems, they describe them as . . . a sign that the Beurs felt no one was listening to them."**

of higher tension. Often, however, their solidarity creates a reaction among the rest of society that further marginalizes them, both socially and economically. As a result, the crisis frequently deepens. The collective perception of injustice among group members repeatedly boils over into violence.

The Suprême NTM, a rap group that made its name in the 1990s, illustrates the combative mood among young urban Beurs. In a song called "What We Expect" ("*Qu'est-ce qu'on attend*"), they call on France "to take account of its crimes," only to announce that it's far too late for that:

> *From now on the street will not forgive*
> *We have nothing to lose for we have*
>   *never had anything*
> *In your place I would not sleep well*
> *The bourgeoisie should tremble,*
>   *the gangsters are in town*
> *Not to party, but to burn the place*
>   *down. . . .*
> *Let's unite and incinerate the system*
> *But why, why are we waiting to burn*
>   *the place down?*

This 1995 song proved prophetic when, in October 2005, the *banlieues* surrounding Paris and more than one hundred other cities saw unprecedented riots, violence, and arson. Although most experts agree that the riots centered around socio-economic problems, they describe them as a breakdown in the French democratic process—a sign that the Beurs felt no one was listening to them.

Implications for Education and Democracy: A Discussion

In many Western countries, religious, ethnic, and economic divides present a growing challenge for the strength of democracy. In response to this challenge, many politicians in Europe warn against splitting societies along ethnic lines and seek policies designed to achieve higher degrees of community cohesion. The banning of the veil in France and other countries was one attempt to address these problems. Similar calls to ban Muslim coverings in Britain, Germany, the Netherlands, and Belgium showed that the secularist opposition to this Muslim tradition was not limited to France. Nor were these anti-veil sentiments confined to countries with a Christian majority. For example, Turkey, a largely Muslim country that aspires to join the European Union, has a strict secular tradition. In the past, Turkish secularists, much like many other European governments, argued that secularism does not allow for a public display of religious symbols. As a result, successive Turkish governments enforced a ban of Islamic veils in universities (traditional headscarves, known in Turkey as baş örtüsü, are largely acceptable). Not surprisingly, however, the new position of Turkey's ruling Justice and Development Party, which has been in power since 2002 and supports *lifting* the ban on veils on campuses, is likely to create an obstacle for the accession of Turkey to the European Union.[83] In sum, these debates in Europe and elsewhere highlight the fact that in many European countries, Islamic symbols and traditions are seen as a threat to the secular state.

Instead of comparing these various discussions, we have chosen to focus on France, where the debate was most public—and because France, more than any other country in Western Europe, stresses assimilation as a path to acceptance. But the debates surrounding the veil affairs in France are instructive in yet another way: they raise fundamental questions about the best ways to accommodate ethnic and religious differences in a democracy.

There are a number of objections secularists must face. Scholar Olivier Roy argues that the first question is whether the conflicts arise because of the very specific idea of *laïcité* in France or whether the expression of religious diversity is anathema to secularism in general. Roy's two-fold definition of *laïcité* may help us wrestle with the question: According to Roy, since 1905, legal *laïcité* has excluded the church from all areas of public life. This does not mean that religions give up their claims to a single truth or to insights that transcend worldly laws and regulations. Rather, they agree to respect the democratic rules of the game and promise not to undermine the rule of law by violent or illegal acts. Many inhabitants of France

"Many inhabitants of France see laïcité as far more than [the separation between state and church]. For them, it expands into an ideology that 'claims to provide a value system common to all citizens.'" —Olivier Roy

see *laïcité* as far more than that. For them, it expands into an ideology that "claims to provide a value system common to all citizens."[84] It does so by expelling religion from the public sphere and limiting it to citizens' private lives, while declaring certain values nonnegotiable.[85]

Critics argue that the second definition is the source of the problem, and that France's ideological secularity is excessive. They argue that France is more than a purely political community, and that its citizens cannot cut themselves off from their religious or ethnic identities. Specifically, critics wonder if this form of secularity violates the rights of those whose religions make specific claims on their public lives, including the wearing of the veil.

Other critics raise deeper questions regarding the wider implications of the pressure to ban the display of the veil in public spaces. What does it mean to integrate a population that's required to give up essential parts of identity? To Ghanaian American philosopher Kwame Anthony Appiah, the French model of secularism/assimilation rings hollow if we expect everyone to be the same:

In a recent New Yorker *cartoon, a dog is speaking to a cat it has chased up a tree: "Okay, here's the deal—I'll stop chasing you if you agree to become a dog." Is this, finally, what neutrality amounts to?*[86]

Educators may also question the message sent to their students when some are prohibited from fully expressing their identity while, at the same time, others can do as they please because the majority has grown accustomed to their community's symbols. Such double standards abound. In Germany, for example, "several regional governments have banned teachers from wearing headscarves since 2003, while continuing to allow the display of Christian and Jewish symbols."[87] Educators warn that such practice can be an obstacle in adolescents' developmental process. Indeed, expressing one identity and learning to take the perspective of another, which are hallmarks of adolescence, are also essential global competencies.

Moreover, adolescents and young adults around the world show time and again that they turn to their community's history and culture to seek meaning and identity.[88] Arguably, banning the veil or any other "ostentatious" religious symbol (and the lack of attention the multiple identities of students receive in public schools) serves to deny at least some students access to such cultural resources. German philosopher Jürgen Habermas claims that the issue is essential for the health of democracy. Religion, he argues, often serves as

"Okay, here's the deal—I'll stop chasing you if you agree to become a dog."

Two students exchange a friendly gesture of support as one returns to school fully veiled. Youths in France are challenging tradition and bridging divides through food, music, and sports at an unprecedented level.

"a source of energy that the person who has a faith taps . . . and thus nurtures his or her entire life."[89] In fact, he continues, "democracy has an interest . . . in unleashing religious voices in the political public sphere, for it cannot know whether secular society would not otherwise cut itself off from key resources for the creation of meaning and identity."[90]

For some people, religion can provide direction, motivation, and inspiration—all of which are essential to keeping democracy alive and authentic.[91] For future citizens, the multiplicity of voices is vitally important. For it is among the competing historical narratives of different communities that citizens are able to find their own vision of their future society.

Some educators also argue that the debate is not really about the headscarves but rather about the denial of the history of North Africans and their relation to France. They further claim that when teachers allow their students to question the national narrative, they tap into adolescents' newly acquired skill to think hypothetically and to view history as manmade rather than an unchangeable, fixed past. Lifelong educator (and

one of Facing History and Ourselves' first teachers) Martin E. Sleeper argues that

the adolescent, unlike the child, is no longer bound to the reality of the past. The reformulation between reality and possibility means that in history the adolescent can understand that what happened did not necessarily have to happen. . . . The adolescent can imagine alternatives, construct different possibilities, and contemplate their outcome.[92]

Moreover, by encouraging students to probe the past, teachers also provide their students with the opportunity to see the past from the perspective of those whose story was written out of the pages of history. Students who take such a perspective can, in turn, address past inequities and imagine a more just future for their societies. Educating active, critical citizens is therefore intimately linked to the multiplicity of histories they encounter.

Joan Wallach Scott, the author of a challenging set of historical reflections on the headscarf debate, explained the question that motivated her work: "Perhaps it's the democratic outcomes I'm interested in more than the principle of secularism itself."[93] She wanted to know whether banning the veil made France more or less democratic. Did insisting on strict secularity draw more people into the democratic process? Or did it alienate them or shut some of them out?

People's desire to participate in the political process depends on their ability to find their common roots and on their ability to voice publicly both individual and group concerns. Indeed, the legitimacy of the democratic process is linked to the ability of all social groups to sit at the national democratic table and to negotiate their rights and responsibilities. In Appiah's words,

> "Secularism is not negotiable," [President] Chirac insisted. I would rather say that secularism is negotiation—a negotiation between respect for individuals and tolerance of the values and practices through which they give meaning to their lives.[94]

It is therefore not at all clear how denying one group's tradition facilitates this sense of belonging that is at the heart of democracy.

Scott argues further that placing so much weight on the idea that Muslims must conform to the ideals of *laïcité* can only lead to trouble. Secularism, she repeats, is not synonymous with democracy;

after all, devoutly secularist ideologies were behind some of the worst crimes in human history—just think of Stalin's Soviet Union and Nazi Germany. Many religious states have fine democratic records (Denmark, Finland, and Iceland all have official state religions to this day), and numerous countries with overwhelming Muslim majorities have secular governments, including Turkey. Scott suggests that far more energy be devoted to maintaining democratic dialogues to promote mutual understanding and respect for differences. Much like Appiah, she argues that the elimination of differences quashes such dialogues, putting an end to the meaningful exchanges that could foster national solidarity.[95] And recent debates about other issues related to the Muslim population indicate that the ban on headscarves did not address many of the underlying tensions in France. These discussions are by no means confined to France. They focus on equal opportunities, the building of new mosques, ethnic profiling and other security measures, citizenship tests and immigration policies, and funding for Muslim schools—debates that defy assertions about the centrality of the head coverings to Europe's contemporary social ills. They may in fact point to deep cultural, ethnic, religious, and economic tensions that only concerted educational efforts and intercultural dialogue could dissolve.

[1] Noah Feldman, "The New Pariahs?" the *New York Times Magazine*, June 22, 2008, *http://www.nytimes.com/2008/06/22/magazine/22wwln-lede-t.html?_r=1&scp=1&sq=Noah%20Feldman&st=nyt&oref=slogin* (accessed June 23, 2008). Among the critics we consulted for this project are José Casanova, John Bowen, Martha Minow, Zvi Ben Dor, Daniel Cohen, Riem Spielhous, Viola Beatrix Georgi, Dan Jones, Jonathan Lawrence, and Rashid Khalidi. We owe them a big debt of gratitude for their help. They bear no responsibility for the content of this book.

[2] For stimulating reflections on this process, see Arjun Appadurai, *Fear of Small Numbers: An Essay on the Geography of Anger* (Durham: Duke University Press, 2006).

[3] José Casanova, "Immigration and the New Religious Pluralism: A European Union/United States Comparison," in Thomas Banchoff (ed.), *Democracy and the New Religious Pluralism* (Oxford: Oxford University Press, 2007), 59. We thank José Casanova for his insightful advice and suggestions.

[4] United Nations Department of Economic and Social Affairs, "International Migration 2006," United Nations Economic and Social Development website, *http://www.un.org/esa/population/publications/2006Migration_Chart/2006IttMig_wallchart.xls* (accessed June 19, 2008).

[5] "Stocks of foreign-born population in selected OECD countries," The Organization for Economic Cooperation and Development website, *http://www.oecd.org/dataoecd/25/55/39331322.xls* (accessed February 11, 2008).

[6] United Nations, Department of Economic and Social Affairs, "International Migration 2006."

[7] Michael Freund, "Say Goodbye to Europe," the *Jerusalem Post*, January 10, 2007, *http://www.jpost.com/servlet/Satellite?cid=1167467696394&pagename=JPost%2FJPArticle%2FShowFull* (accessed June 15, 2007).

[8] Tariq Modood, *Multiculturalism: A Civic Idea* (Cambridge: Polity, 2007), 4.

[9] Beate Winkler, "Looking Forward to the Future: Europe's Societies Are Undergoing Change," *UN Chronicle* online, n.d., *http://www.un.org/Pubs/chronicle/2007/issue3/0307p32.html* (accessed June 20, 2008); "Mosque with 25-metre Minarets to be Constructed in Marseille," the *Earth Times*, November 22, 2007, *http://www.earthtimes.org/articles/show/146537.html* (accessed June 20, 2008); "Selection of Cities and Neighborhoods to Monitor," EU Monitoring and Advocacy Program website, *http://www.eumap.org/topics/minority/reports/eumuslims/methodology/cities* (accessed June 20, 2008).

[10] Walter Laqueur, *The Last Days of Europe: Epitaph for an Old Continent* (New York: St. Martin's Press, 2007).

[11] Tariq Modood, "Remaking multiculturalism after 7/7," *Open Democracy*, September 29, 2005, *http://www.opendemocracy.net/conflict-terrorism/multiculturalism_2879.jsp* (accessed December 5, 2007).

[12] For an overview of the Dutch model, see Jane Kramer, "The Dutch Model: Multiculturalism and Muslim Immigrants," the *New Yorker*, April 3, 2006, 60–67.

[13] Ibid., 63.

[14] Olivier Roy, *Secularism Confronts Islam*, trans. George Holoch (New York: Columbia University Press, 2007), x.

[15] Adam B. Seligman, *Religion and Human Rights: Conflict or Convergence* (Hollis: Hollis Publishing Company, 2005), 4.

[16] Angelique Chrisafis, "France Rejects Muslim Woman Over Radical Practice of Islam," the *Guardian*, (July 12, 2008), *http://www.guardian.co.uk/world/2008/jul/12/france.islam.*

[17] Norma Cliare Moruzzi, "A Problem with Headscarves: Contemporary Complexities of Political and Social Identity," *Political Theory* 22 (1994): 657–58.

[18] John R. Bowen, *Why the French Don't Like Headscarves: Islam, the State, and Public Space* (Princeton: Princeton University Press, 2007), 87–92.

[19] The relationship between the two groups has worsened considerably since 2001. See Jean-Marc Dreyfus and Jonathan Laurence, "Anti-Semitism in France," Brookings Institute website, *http://www.brookings.edu/~/media/Files/rc/articles/2002/0514france_dreyfus/dreyfus.pdf* (accessed November 15, 2007).

[20] Riva Kastoryano, "France's Veil Affair," *Inroads* (Summer 2004), Find Articles website, *http://www.findarticles.com/p/articles/mi_qa4014/is_200407/ai_n9467219* (accessed January 25, 2007).

21 Moruzzi, "A Problem with Headscarves," 659–64. For the feminist perspective, see Fadela Amara with Sylvia Zappi, *Breaking the Silence: French Women's Voices from the Ghetto*, trans. Helen Harden Chenut (Berkeley: University of California Press, 2006), 73–74, 98–102, 154.

22 The court added, "Such freedom does not, however, extend to permitting students to wear religious symbols that . . . would constitute an act of pressure, provocation, proselytism or propaganda, or detract from the dignity or freedom of the student or other members of the educational community . . . or disrupt the establishment or normal operation of the public service." Cited in Laura Barnett, "Freedom of Religion and Religious Symbols in the Public Sphere," 2006, Library of Parliament (Canada) website, *http://www.parl.gc.ca/information/library/PRBpubs/prb0441-e.htm* (accessed November 15, 2007); Bruce Crumley, "Faith and Fury," *Time*, November 2, 2003, *http://www.time.com/time/magazine/article/0,9171,901031110-536181-2,00.html* (accessed December 21, 2007). The Conseil d'Etat and the French Ministry of Education left it up to school principals to interpret the ruling.

23 Bowen, *Why the French Don't Like Headscarves*, 86–87. For a comparison to a United States school in Maine, see Hazel Rose Markus, "Identity Matters: Ethnicity, Race, and the American Dream," in Martha Minow, Richard A. Shweder, and Hazel Rose Markus (eds.), *Just Schools: Pursuing Equality in Societies of Difference* (New York: The Russell Sage Foundation, 2008), 63–100.

24 James F. Hollifield, "Ideas, Institutions, and Civil Society: On the Limits of Immigration Control in France," *Research and Seminars*, 4, no. 4 (1989), *http://migration.ucdavis.edu/rs/more.php?id=70_0_3_0* (accessed January 25, 2007).

25 Joan Wallach Scott, *The Politics of the Veil* (Princeton: Princeton University Press, 2007), 27.

26 Meira Levinson, "Liberalism Versus Democracy? Schooling Private Citizens in the Public Square," *British Journal of Political Science* 27 (1997): 352.

27 Jocelyn Cesari et al., *Muslims in Western Europe after 9/11: Why the term Islamophobia is more a predicament than an explanation*, Challenge: Liberty and Security website, November 22, 2006, *http://libertysecurity.org/article1167.html*, 7 (accessed November 15, 2007).

28 Richard Wolin, "Veiled Intolerance," April 9, 2007, the *Nation* online, *http://www.thenation.com/doc/20070409/wolin* (accessed on November 15, 2007).

29 Etienne Balibar, "Dissonances within *Laïcité*," *Constellations* 11 (2004): 354.

30 Caitlin Killian, "The Other Side of the Veil: North African Women in France Respond to the Headscarf Affair," *Gender and Society* 17, no. 4 (2003): 577.

31 Adrien Katherine Wing and Monica Smith, "Critical Race Feminism Lifts the Veil? Muslim Women, France, and the Headscarf Ban," *UC Davis Law Review* (2006): 765. For a 2008 update on this debate, see Sylbia Poggioli's audio journal entitled "French Muslim Women Forge New Islam, Activism," National Public Radio website, *http://www.npr.org/templates/story/story.php?storyId=18119226* (accessed February 5, 2008).

32 Nicolas Sarkozy, "Twentieth Annual Meeting of the Union of France's Islamic Organizations" (speech, Le Borget, Paris, France, April 19, 2003), *http://www.ambafrance-us.org/news/statmnts/2003/islam041903.asp* (accessed November 11, 2007).

33 John R. Bowen, "Muslims and Citizens: France's Headscarf Controversy," *Boston Review* (February/March 2004), 31.

34 T. Jeremy Gunn, "Under God But Not the Scarf: The Founding Myths of Religious Freedom in the United States and *Laïcité* in France," *Journal of Church and State* 7 (2004): 7. Later, the Socialist Party also "joined arms with the conservatives in a cause that had the support of a majority of the French population" (Bowen, "Muslims and Citizens: France's Headscarf Controversy," 31).

35 Bowen, *Why the French Don't Like Headscarves*, 110–11.

36 Jacques Chirac, "Respecting the Principle of Secularism in the Republic" (speech, Paris, France, December 17, 2003), *http://www.elysee.fr/elysee/elysee.fr/anglais/speeches_and_documents/2003/speech_by_jacques_chirac_president_of_the_republic_on_respecting_the_principle_of_secularism_in_the_republic-excerpts.2675.html* (accessed December 20, 2007).

37 Chirac, "Respecting the Principle of Secularism in the Republic."

38 Scott, *Politics of the Veil*, 41.

39 Jonathan Laurence and Justin Vaisse, *Integrating Islam: Political and Religious Challenges in Contemporary France* (Washington, D.C.: The Brookings Institution, 2006), 139–40.

40 Count Stanislas-Marie-Adélaide de Clermont-Tonnerre, "Speech on Religious Minorities and Questionable Professions," December 23, 1789, Center for History and New Media website, *http://chnm.gmu.edu/revolution/d/284/* (accessed on June 13, 2008).

[41] Scott, *Politics of the Veil*, 99.

[42] In reality, the same source continued, getting rid of the "unwholesome" influence of the Catholic church was a vital step in reforming the Republic's schools. See "School Reform in France," the *New York Times*, August 23, 1880, *http://query.nytimes.com/gst/abstract.html?res=9D0CE3DB153BE033A25750C2A96E9C94619FD7CF* (accessed April 22, 2008).

[43] Scott, *Politics of the Veil*, 99.

[44] Jules François Camille Ferry, "Speech Before the French Chamber of Deputies, March 28, 1884," *Discours et Opinions de Jules Ferry*, ed. Paul Robiquet (Paris: Armand Colin & Cie., 1897), trans. Ruth Kleinman, Modern History Sourcebook website, *http://www.fordham.edu/halsall/mod/1884ferry.html* (accessed August, 13, 2008).

[45] Alice L. Coklin, *A Mission to Civilize: The Republican Idea of Empire in France and West Africa*, 1895–1930 (Stanford: Stanford University Press, 1997), 13.

[46] For an extended treatment of the ideology behind these and other racist ideologies, see *Race and Membership in American History: The Eugenics Movement* (Brookline: Facing History and Ourselves Foundation, Inc., 2002).

[47] Levison, "Liberalism Versus Democracy?" 352.

[48] Leslie J. Limage, "Education and Muslim Identity: The Case of France," *Comparative Education* 36, no. 1 (2000): 79. We would like to thank Leslie Limage for her contributions to our research.

[49] Richard Hatcher and Dominique Leblond, "Education Action Zones and Zones d'Education Prioritaires." Paper presented at the conference on Traveling Policy/Local Spaces: Globalisation, Identities and Education Policy in Europe, organized by the Department of Education, Keele University, June 27–29, 2001, *http://www.keele.ac.uk/depts/ed/events/conf-pdf/cPaperHatcher.pdf* (accessed February 12, 2008); Roland Bénabou et al., "The French Zones d'Education Prioritaire: Much Ado about Nothing?" Discussion Paper No. 5085, May 2005, Center for Economics Policy Research website, *www.princeton.edu/~rbenabou/CEPR-DP5085.pdf* (accessed November 15, 2007).

[50] Educators such as Jean Louis Auduc (director of L'IUFM de Créteil) have been advocating for a more open approach to religion and ethnic identity. See Jean-Louis Auduc, "Forging a Common Sense of Belonging: Respecting the Diversity of Identities," *Prospects* 36, no. 3 (September 2006): 319–326; cf. Auduc, *Éducation civique, 4e: Libertés et droits, justice, Europe* (Paris: Hachette, 2002); Trica Danielle Keaton, *Muslim Girls and the Other France: Race, Identity Politics, and Social Exclusion* (Bloomington: Indiana University Press, 2006), 129–30.

[51] Keaton, *Muslim Girls and the Other France*, 113.

[52] Jytte Klausen, *The Islamic Challenge: Politics and Religion in Western Europe* (Oxford: Oxford University Press, 2005), 136.

[53] Richard L. Derderian, *North Africans in Contemporary France: Becoming Visible* (New York: Palgrave Macmillan, 2004), 8–9.

[54] Thomas Deltombe, *L'islam imaginaire: La construction médiatique de l'Islamophobie en France 1975–2005* (Paris: La Découverte 2005), 232. Peyrefitte published this conversation with de Gaulle in his 1994 book *Ainsi Parlait de Gaulle*, a biography of the French general and president.

[55] Lawrence and Vaisse, *Integrating Islam*, 7.

[56] The idea of the French melting pot (*le creuset français*) was proposed in 1988 in Gérard Noiriel, *The French Melting Pot: Immigration, Citizenship, and National Identity*, trans. Geoffroy de Laforcade (Minneapolis: University of Minnesota Press, 1996).

[57] Eugen Weber, *Peasants into Frenchmen: The Modernization of Rural France, 1870–1914* (Stanford: Stanford University Press, 1976).

[58] Derderian, *North Africans in Contemporary France*, 6.

[59] Derderian, *North Africans in Contemporary France*, 8. These shantytowns in France were called *bidonvilles*.

[60] Tahar Ben Jelloun, *French Hospitality: Racism and North African Immigrants*, trans. Barbara Bray (New York: Columbia University Press, 1999), 12.

[61] Ben Jelloun, *French Hospitality: Racism and North African Immigrants*, 14.

[62] Richard Alba and Roxane Silberman, "Decolonization Immigrations and the Social Origins of the Second Generation: The Case of North Africans in France," *International Migration Review* 36, no. 4 (2002): 1169–93. A recent survey of second-generation North African French residents indicated that in terms of reading and other standard educational measurements, they lag well behind the native population. Reading and math skills are considered good predictors of future social status and income. See "Educational Outcomes for Children of Immigrants," Organization for Economic Cooperation and Development website, 2007, *http://lysander.sourceoecd.org/vl=1629100/cl=57/nw=1/rpsv/factbook/12-03-01.htm* (accessed February 11, 2008).

[63] "Stock of Foreign-Born Population by Country of Birth," The Organization for Economic Cooperation and Development website, 2007, *http://www.oecd.org/dataoecd/26/42/39332415.xls* (accessed February 11, 2008).

[64] Derderian, *North Africans in Contemporary France*, 147–49.

[65] Albert Memmi walks us through such a neighborhood:
In the small back alleys are places of worship, where exotic imams exhort their followers to respect the Quran and maintain solidarity with other Muslims. There are the sympathetic cafés, where while drinking tea or playing the pinball machines, watching a North African, Egyptian, or Saudi Arabian television station, events are discussed, shared hopes and fears are aired, and rumors are exchanged. There are the butcher shops with signs in Arabic characters, selling ritual, or "halal," cuts of meat. With all the disorder of the [market place], grocers sell the foods one ate as a child, the imported spices, grains, vegetables, and fruits.
Albert Memmi, *Decolonization and the Decolonized*, trans. Robert Bononno (Minneapolis: University of Minnesota Press, 2006), 83.

[66] Kacel Karim, "Banlieue," trans. Anna L. Romer, *Banlieue*, compact disc, EMI 1998.

[67] Ben Jelloun, *French Hospitality*, 91.

[68] We thank Daniel Cohen for this and many other invaluable suggestions and comments.

[69] "Il y a vingt ans, la 'marche des beurs,'" BLADI.net (December 3, 2003), *http://www.bladi.net/2656-il-y-a-vingt-ans-la-marche-des-beurs.html* (accessed April 17, 2008); "Dix ans après leur première marche les Beurs veulent toujours l'égalité," *L'Humanité* (December 3, 1993), *http://www.humanite.fr/1993-12-03_Articles_Dix-ans-apres-leur-premiere-marche-les-Beurs-veulent-toujours-l* (accessed April 17, 2008).

[70] Ben Jelloun, *French Hospitality*, 107.

[71] Frank Buijs, "Homegrown Warriors," unpublished manuscript, 2007, Chap. 7.

[72] Cf. Paul A. Silverstein, "Sporting Faith: Islam, Soccer, and the French Nation-State," *Social Text* 65, No. 18, (2000): 33–42.

[73] Tony Karon, "The Head Butt Furor: A Window on Europe's Identity Crisis," *Time Magazine* online, July 13, 2006, *http://www.time.com/time/world/article/0,8599,1213502,00.html* (accessed November 19, 2007).

[74] Valérie Orlando, "From Rap to Räi in the Mixing Bowl: Beur Hip-Hop Culture and *Banlieue* Cinema in Urban France," *Journal of Popular Culture* 36, no. 3 (2003): 400.

[75] André J. M. Prévos, "The Evolution of French Rap Music and Hip Hop Culture in the 1980s and 1990s," the *French Review* 69 (1996): 716.

[76] Stéphanie Giry, "France and Its Muslims," *Foreign Affairs* 85 (2006), 87.

[77] "Muslims in Europe: Economic Worries Top Concern about Religious and Cultural Identity," Pew Global Attitudes Project website, *http://pewglobal.org/reports/display.php?ReportID=254* (accessed November 16, 2007).

[78] Laurence and Vaisse, *Integrating Islam*, 44.

[79] See the Pew report entitled *The Great Divide: How Westerners and Muslims View Each Other,* Pew Global Attitudes Project website, *Europe's Muslims More Moderate, http://pewglobal.org/reports/display.php?ReportID=253* (accessed November 16, 2007).

[80] Keaton, *Muslim Girls and the Other France*, 40.

[81] Adam Sage, "Headscarf Ban Is Judged Success as Hostility Fades," the *Times* online, September 5, 2005, *http://www.timesonline.co.uk/tol/news/world/europe/article562622.ece* (accessed November 16, 2007).

[82] Supreme NTM, "Qu'est-Ce Qu'on Attend," trans. Daniel Cohen, *Paris sous les bombes*, compact disc, MSI music 1999.

[83] Antonia Ruiz Jimenez, "Turkey's Headscarf Legislation: The Negative Impact on EU Accession," The Washington Institute for Near East Policy website (May 5, 2008), *http://www.washingtoninstitute.org/templateC05.php?CID=2830* (accessed August 7, 2008).

[84] Roy, *Secularism Confronts Islam*, xii.

[85] Ibid., 38.

[86] Kwame Anthony Appiah, "The Limits of Being Liberal," *Philosophia Africana* 8, no. 2 (2005): 95.

[87] Antonia Ruiz Jimenez, "Turkey's Headscarf Legislation: The Negative Impact on EU Accession."

[88] Martin E. Sleeper, "The Uses of History in Adolescence," *Youth and Society* 4 (1973): 261.

[89] Jürgen Habermas, "Religion in the Public Sphere," *Philosophia Africana* 8, no. 2 (2005): 102.

[90] Ibid., 103.

[91] Habermas further argues that the legitimacy of the democratic process is at stake, because democracies are founded on such dialogue. All parties must have equal access to the political process, and all must agree to the protocols and language used in political life—this is the opposite of dogmatism, coercion, and violence. In his words, "The citizens of a democratic community owe one another good reasons for their public political [actions]" (103).

[92] Martin E. Sleeper, "A Developmental Framework for History Education in Adolescence," School Review 84 (1975): 102.

[93] Scott, *The Politics of the Veil*, 94.

[94] Appiah, "The Limits of Being Liberal," 95, 97.

[95] Scott, *The Politics of the Veil*, 175–83.

Part Two
Primary Documents

"Schools must be places of understanding,
of knowledge of other cultures. . . .
The challenge facing the inclusive
school is therefore not to oppose cultures
and traditions, but to start from the
principle that each culture contributes
a part of the whole . . . in order to forge
a common feeling of belonging that does
not deny the diversity of identities."
– Jean-Louis Auduc, French educator

What Does It Mean to Be French?

"More than 200 years after the French Revolution, many people point to the principles of liberty, equality, and brotherhood (liberté, égalité, fraternité) as the glue that holds the country together."

As their country becomes more diverse, people in France have been questioning what it means to be French. More than 200 years after the French Revolution, many people point to the principles of liberty, equality, and brotherhood (*liberté, égalité, fraternité*) as the glue that holds the country together. But in reality, not everybody who lives in France feels welcome. French identity is rooted, at least in some people's minds, in French history, religion, and culture. Charles de Gaulle (1890–1970), the French leader who is credited with rebuilding the country after the horrors of World War II, described French identity this way:

> It is very good that there are yellow Frenchmen, black Frenchmen, brown Frenchmen. They prove that France is open to all races and that she has a universal mission. But they must remain a small minority. Otherwise, France would no longer be France. We are after all primarily a European people of the white race, our culture Greek and Latin, our religion Christian.[1]

General de Gaulle greets crowds in Algiers in 1958. De Gaulle was elected president of France in 1958 to bring an end to the Algerian War of Independence, which he did in 1962. Algeria and North Africa were the source of much of France's initial immigration in the period following World War II.

But France's population is no longer as homogeneous as it used to be—France has both the largest Muslim and Jewish populations in Europe.

Moreover, while de Gaulle proudly proclaimed France's Christian heritage, today many French people stress the importance of secularity (*laïcité*)—a strict separation of religion from public life—as a way to ensure equal opportunities for all. Recently this tradition seemed to be in conflict with the needs and cultural expectations of France's Muslim minorities. In December 2003, French President Jacques Chirac addressed these tensions and spoke about the French model of integration, which stresses assimilation into French culture and language:

A land of ideas and principles, France is an open, hospitable and generous country. United around a unique heritage from which they derive strength and pride, the French people enjoy a rich diversity. A diversity which is accepted and is at the heart of our identity . . . [including a] diversity of beliefs . . . diversity of regions. . . .

And of course diversity of those women and men who, in each generation, have come to join the national community and for whom France was first an ideal before becoming a homeland. . . .

One thing is certain: the answer to these concerns does not lie in the . . . withdrawal into oneself or one's community. On the contrary, it lies in the affirmation of our wish to live together, bolstering the common [patriotic] fervor, in remaining true to our history and our values.[2]

Terre d'idées et de principes, la France est une terre ouverte, accueillante et généreuse. Uni autour d'un héritage singulier qui fait sa force et sa fierté, le peuple français est riche de sa diversité. Une diversité assumée et qui est au coeur de notre identité.

Diversité des croyances . . . Diversité des régions . . . Et bien sûr, diversité de ces femmes et de ces hommes qui, à chaque génération, sont venus rejoindre la communauté nationale et pour qui la France a d'abord été un idéal avant de devenir une patrie. . . .

Une chose est sûre: la réponse à ces interrogations n'est pas dans l'infiniment petit du repli sur soi ou du communautarisme. Elle est au contraire dans l'affirmation de notre désir de vivre ensemble, dans la consolidation de l'élan commun, dans la fidélité à notre histoire et à nos valeurs.[3]

The success of novelist and researcher Azouz Begag is in many ways symbolic of successful integration. Begag's memoir of life in an immigrant neighborhood, *Shantytown Kid* (English translation, 2007), has been commonly taught in French schools. In 2005, he was appointed France's first Minister for Equal Opportunities. He was France's first ever cabinet member of North African immigrant origin. Despite his success, he has been continually reminded that, in the eyes of some, he isn't really French. In a recent work addressing the political and ethnic landscape of France today, Begag writes:

My name is Azouz, diminutive of Aziz. I am a French citizen, born in the third arrondissement of Lyon, and regard myself as the spiritual son of the 1789 Declaration of the Rights of Man and of the Citizen . . . I'm nearly fifty, I'm getting "old," and by the same token I have no need to worry about the police excess or racist insults from which I suffered so much as a teenager in the housing projects where I lived. . . .

Then, one evening after dark, a young woman in a police uniform waved me down, stopped me, and came up to my car. I can't now remember whether I bade her good evening. In any event, in what seemed like a panic-stricken voice she abruptly asked me whether I could see any "fog" outside . . . So I looked through my windshield, and stuck my head out the window, but saw no trace of fog. "You don't see any fog?" the young woman repeated. "No, sorry . . ." I wished I could have helped and was trying to offer to do so when she interrupted me and barked: "Well, switch off your fog lamps!"

Despite his success, Azouz Begag, French Minister for Equal Opportunities, has been continually reminded that, in the eyes of some, he isn't really French.

© Philippe Merle/AFP/Getty Images

For a few seconds I was dazed. I couldn't understand what was going on. My mind oscillated between thinking I must have misheard and fearing I heard only too well. She must have been twenty-five. Sheepishly I came to the conclusion that I had correctly heard what she had shouted at me. My hands started fumbling around the dashboard in search of the . . . fog-light switch, which I had, of course, never used. She pointed abruptly to the switch, as if to say: "Is this car really yours?" I pressed the button, and an orange light went out. She then invited me unceremoniously to move on. I drove off. Then I stalled. I could see her shaking her head at the sight of such an incompetent driver. Fortunately I managed to start the motor again. After driving a hundred yards, I burst out laughing. OK, it was a nervous laugh. But I realized that I had refrained from telling her that I was an advisor to the minister of the interior . . . with the mission of promoting equal opportunities in the police service.

When I got back home, in a narrow street in the Arab quarter of Lyon, I still felt agitated. I felt bitter and sick. Why had the young policewomen talked to me so discourteously? What image of me could she have had in her head to talk so disrespectfully to a citizen such as me? [4]

Connections

1. What does it mean to be French? What words, images, and ideas do you associate with French national identity?

2. What is the "glue" that holds your country together? What words and symbols are linked to your country? What do they say about the nation's identity and its values?

3. How did de Gaulle define France's national identity? What changes in this definition did you notice in Chirac's speech?

4. How do you explain the police office officer's response to Begag? What lesson do you think he learned from this encounter?

5. Have you ever been in a situation like the one Begag describes? How did you feel? What words does Begag use to help you understand how he felt?

6. Do you think Begag should have told the officer about his position in the government? If he did, what would it have accomplished?

7. How might the experiences of integration change an immigrant's identity? How might immigrants change the communities into which they migrate?

8. What do you regard as your community? What makes somebody a member of your community? Has anyone ever made you question your ties to your community? If so, how did it make you feel?

[1] Quoted in Thomas Deltombe, *L'islam imaginaire: La construction médiatique de l'islamophobie en France 1975–2005,* (Paris: La Découverte, 2005), 232.

[2] Jacques Chirac, "Principle of Secularism in the Republic" (speech, Paris, France, December 17, 2003), Embassy of France in the United States, *http://www.info-france-usa.org/news/statmnts/2003/chirac_secularism121703.asp* (accessed December 12, 2007).

[3] Discours prononcé par M. Jacques Chirac, Président de la République, relatif au respect du principe de laïcité dans la République, Fil Info France, December 17, 2003, *http://www.fil-info-france.com/actualites-monde/discours-chirac-loi-laicite.htm* (accessed April 9, 2008).

[4] Azouz Begag, *Ethnicity and Equality: France in the Balance* (Lincoln: University of Nebraska Press, 2007) 5, 8–9.

Integration and Exclusion

"How are we supposed to be integrated into France when we are French?"

The majority of Muslim immigrants came to France as "guest workers" after World War II, during the booming economy of the 1950s and 1960s. They came from France's North African colonies and, to a lesser extent, from Turkey and sub-Saharan Africa. These workers served in the least attractive jobs and were expected to return to their home countries after their work was completed (other European countries also saw similar migration from their former colonies). But despite a severe economic crisis in the mid-1970s and restrictive immigration laws, the French soon realized that the entry of mostly Arab immigrants was not going to stop and that these immigrants were in France to stay. Although France does not keep public records about religious identity, it is believed that close to five million Muslims live in France today.

Roughly a decade later, in the 1980s, the sons and daughters of the first generation of immigrants came of age and began to assert their identity in France. In an effort to shake off old stereotypes, they called themselves Beurs (a slang inversion of the word *Arabe* in French) and demanded equality. But, like their parents, they struggled to assimilate into an inhospitable environment.

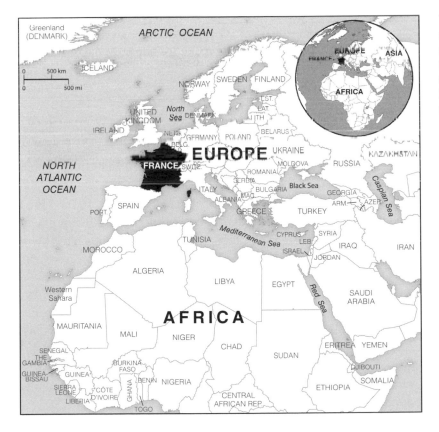

This map shows the proximity of Europe and Africa. The connections between the two continents go back many centuries, but immigration from North Africa to Europe increased dramatically after World War II

Social exclusion was at work as well: The government settled new immigrants and their families on the outskirts of France's big cities and later gave them small and crowded apartments in housing projects. Recently, the *banlieues*, or suburban ghettos, have become known for crime, social unrest, and unemployment (which is estimated in these suburbs at 40 percent). In the 1980s, when the Beur generation began building its community's institutions—religious, political, and commercial—its efforts were often met with hostility and resentment. Many experienced an identity crisis: Were they French, or did they belong to the countries their parents came from? Were they primarily Maghrebian, Arab, Muslim, or French?

Houria (last name not given) was three months old when her family moved from Algeria to Lyon in 1954. She grew up between the first and second generations, and she struggled with the conflicts sparked by her Arab appearance in French society.

Houria works as an assistant accountant in Paris and lives in a studio apartment by herself. During her interview with the novelist and essayist Tahar Ben Jelloun, she talked about the immigrant's struggle to find a home:

No, I really don't want to go to Algeria. It's the last place I'd go to. Why? Nothing attracts me there. . . . I'd be on my guard all the time there. Here, apart from the cops in the metró, I don't have to be on my guard. Here I know what to do, what's expected of me. I know that if anything happens to me there'll be people who'll help me. . . .

In '68 I wanted to go on a demonstration with my friends. My father said, "Do you really think you're at home in France? What has what's been going on here got to do with you?" . . . I remember it well. He was scandalized. I soon faced the facts: no, I wasn't French. Though I don't feel Algerian anymore. And when I'm with French people I feel we haven't much in common, either. Maybe just the lifestyle. Still, I always hang out with the Arabs, not the French. . . .

My father thought he was doing the right thing [emigrating with his family to France]. But he really goofed! He wanted to give us an education—in the first place, to make sure we went to school. But now he knows he made a mistake: none of his children want to go back to Algeria. And it's his fault if we don't speak Arabic properly. At home we spoke half Arabic and half French. My mother? . . . I believe she thinks it's best to take French nationality. But we don't talk about that sort of thing at home. She's realized that, even for her, Algeria is a problem. She's always glad to come back to France after the vacation. It's true! What sort of a life is there in Algeria for an Arab woman who's lived in France for twenty-five years? . . .

My future? I've no idea. I can't see it clearly. Yes, I can see a house, with doors and windows and furniture, but I can't see what country it's in. Whenever I try to make out the actual country the whole thing disappears. I sometimes think about Canada or Australia. . . . No, it's just as well to be stateless. But do they exist—people without a country? Where do they go to? Personally, I need a country—but a country where they don't ask about my family tree, where they don't want to know where I'm from and why I'm dark-skinned. Where they don't wonder if there are any schools and motorcars where I come from. . . .

> No, no—I won't become French. . . . And I'll tell you why. Because we are the Jews of immigration, and I'm afraid, yes, afraid, that some day the French will do to us what they did to the Jews during the last war. . . . There are thousands and thousands of us that the immigration program didn't bargain for. And I, with my background, I'm only a drop in the ocean.[1]

Many believe that France's identity is challenged from both inside and out. From the inside, some fear that in the process of asserting their culture and religion, the Muslims in France will fragment their country's identity. From the outside, many fear that a more religious generation of Muslims will prefer ties with Islamic communities outside France. In fact, they are French citizens. But while young Muslims in Europe want to retain their identity, they wish to be integrated, as well.

Many second-generation migrants in France ask, "How are we supposed to be integrated into France when we are French?" Zebda, a popular Raï group, captures some of these feelings in a song called "I Don't Think It's Going to Be Possible" ("*Je crois pas que ça va être possible*"). The song begins at the door of a nightclub:

> "Please, do come in sir, your presence would be an honor"
> No, I'm just kidding, it doesn't work like that
> In front of a nightclub, I'm always at the mercy
> Of an idiot who targets me and says:
> (Chorus)
> "I don't think it's going to be possible
> Just not gonna work"

Raï music originated from the Bedouin culture in Algeria and is sung in Arabic or French. In this case, the name of the band is important. *zebda* means "butter" in Arabic, a play on the term *Beur*, which, when spelled *beurre*, means "butter" in French.

Connections

1. Many immigrants in France have come from former French colonies. How does that history complicate the relationship between them and the European French?

2. Do countries have an obligation to integrate "guest workers"? What about citizens whose parents were immigrants? What can countries do to foster integration?

3. Create an identity chart for Houria. What words does she use to describe herself? What changes can occur in her identity? What events and influences may cause changes in Houria's chart? (For more information on this activity, see *Facing History and Ourselves: Holocaust and Human Behavior*, Chapter One.)

4. Compare Houria's feelings about home with those of her parents. How does she feel about her French identity? What does she mean when she says that she feels "stateless"?

5. What does Houria mean when she compares the experience of Arab immigrants in France with that of the Jews before and during World War II? What connections is she making?

6. Would you consider the children of immigrants to be French? If so, why? How could you answer children of immigrants who ask, "How are we supposed to become integrated into France when we are French?" What issues do they raise about the way people define French identity?

7. What is the main complaint expressed in the Zebda song? How does it represent the challenges young Muslims face in France?

8. Have you ever been excluded because of your identity? What was the situation? What did you do about it?

Excerpted from *French Hospitality: Racism and North African Immigrants*, translated by Barbara Bray. Copyright © 1999 Columbia University Press. Reprinted with permission of the publisher.

---

[1] Tahar Ben Jelloun, *French Hospitality: Racism and North African Immigrants*, trans. Barbara Bray (New York: Columbia University Press, 1999), 92–94.

The Veil and a New Muslim Identity

"I function as a barometer of the popularity of Muslims."

Many second- and third-generation immigrants from North Africa, feeling neither French nor foreign, see religion as an important part of their identity. Often, these young people have never formally learned about Islam, either because their parents stress the importance of assimilation or because they believed their children would pick up the tradition in the same way they did as children in North Africa. Therefore, many teenagers turn to the local mosque, the Internet, or neighborhood Islamic bookstores to learn more about Islam.[1]

Souad (last name not given) is part of this generation. She was born in France, shortly after her parents arrived from Algeria. She was not brought up to be especially religious, nor does she speak much Arabic. As a sign of her religious commitment, she recently began to wear the veil. In the following interview, Souad describes the journey she undertook:

> Once I got to high school, friends told me about my religion, [and] I discovered an aspect I did not know; I studied, read books, [and] I found that enriching.
>
> It was clear to me that the headscarf was an obligation, and I felt the need to please our Creator; it was in that spirit that I wanted to wear it, but the social conditions at high school presented problems. I had to prepare to be rejected by others. I studied my *bac* [the all-important exam at the end of one's studies at school] and practiced my religion, but the *voile* [veil] was another thing. I always did my prayer, that's something very important for Muslims, and I am proud of myself there. But there was always that desire to go higher in faith, to go closer to the Creator, to please him. So I put on a small hair band so that people would get used to it, because before I wore mini skirts, long hair, but never drank alcohol. In effect I was a bit of a tomboy and hung out with guys, who considered me their little sister and made sure I did not veer toward drugs and night clubs.
>
> One day I decided to become a woman, not a boy, and I changed my behavior because I had been very aggressive. . . . I realized that it is hard to live in society as a woman, because there is a lot of sexism. . . . So, to return to the zigzag, my behavior as a woman, the fact that God asked me to do certain things, so I decided to go in that direction while adapting myself to the society where I live, and I succeed [in] this, for when I am at work I wear the scarf not like I have it now but on top, swirled around like the Africans [makes gesture around her head]. That seems to work. I began wearing it as an intern and it worked. This shows that there are still people who are very tolerant. They knew me before and after the *foulard* [the veil], and their attitude did not change. They saw that my work did not change, even got better, and one said, if anyone criticizes you let me know and I will take care of it. I found that touching.[2]

While for Souad the decision to wear the veil was religious, some believe that young people's decision to wear the veil is as much a reaction against feeling excluded as it is a rebellion against their parents' attempts to fit in. Fariba (last name not given) was born in France, grew up in Algeria, and returned to study in France in 2001 as a young adult. She began wearing the veil, or *hijab*, at age 15 as a part of her religious beliefs. In an interview conducted with anthropologist John Bowen sometime after the 9/11 terrorist attacks in the United States, she argues that how she is seen is based on what is happening in the news:

> Sometimes even when I have not been listening to the news, I know what has happened by watching how people regard me. On September 11th [2001], I returned home from work, turned on the television and saw the catastrophe. I was shocked like everyone else. The next morning, Wednesday, I had almost forgotten what had happened, I took the train to work, and the looks I got from others reminded me that it was the 12th, of what happened the day before. At first I did not understand, I looked myself over, to see if there was something wrong with my clothes, what did I do? And then I made the connection. . . .
>
> The other time it happened to me, it was when there was a French ship blown up, I had not heard about it, and I saw a great deal of aggression in people's stares, and said to myself I had better read a newspaper right away, and I saw the explanation. I function as a barometer of the popularity of Muslims. When there were sympathetic looks it was between the two votes for the president [in April–May 2002], when [right-wing nationalist politician] Jean-Marie Le Pen had done well, they felt guilty, and so in the subway if I was jostled a bit, people would say "Oh, excuse me, ma'am," as if to say, "I did not vote for Le Pen." So in some sense, I have never been spit on or struck or yelled at but I see a lot in those looks.[3]

Fadela Amara, an activist-turned-politician, has protested racism and discrimination against immigrants (especially women) in France for many years. She warns that the headscarf is becoming the symbol of a militant Islam that poses a danger to French democracy. Amara, who was born to Algerian parents and grew up in an immigrant neighborhood, offers her own explanation as to why young women wear headscarves:

French author and feminist Fadela Amara (left) attends a party in Paris in 2008 with Rachida Dati, French Minister of Justice (right), one of the most prominent Muslim figures in France. Amara is currently serving as the French Junior Minister for Urban Affairs and is heading several initiatives aimed at improving life in the *banlieues*. Many French Muslims disapprove of her strong stance against the political use of religion.

Among the young women in the projects there are those who seek recognition in a . . . return to ethnic community life and in particular by returning to Islam, for their identity. Some of them wear the headscarf by choice in the spirit of religious practice. But others have been subjected to pressures . . . from parents, religious leaders, or the [people in the housing] projects. As someone who is very attached to fundamental freedoms, I think religious practice is legitimate when it is a personal choice, without pressure or constraint, but above all when it respects the norms of secular society.

It is possible, in fact, to distinguish different categories of young women who wear the headscarf. First of all, there are those who wear it because they believe that the fact that they practice their religion affords them a legitimate existence. . . . They wear the headscarf as a banner.

But there are many young women who, forbidden any outward display of femininity, wear the headscarf as armor, supposed to protect them from male aggression. Indeed, women who wear the headscarf are never bothered by young [Muslim] men, who lower their eyes in front of them; covered by the headscarf, these girls are in their view untouchable. . . .[4]

Amara believes that something else is at stake, beyond issues of identity:

[There is a] third category of women who wear the headscarf. . . . In general, these are women who attend university and . . . fight for a social project that is dangerous for our democracy. These are not disturbed kids, troubled or searching for an identity, who wear the headscarf because it shows they belong to a community. No, these are real militants! They often begin their justification for wearing the headscarf by explaining that, in their view, it is part of a process of emancipation. It bothers me to hear the talk about freedom of expression because behind this symbol is a [plan to create] a different society than our own: a fascist-like society that has nothing to do with democracy.[5]

Connections

1. Why do you think so many second- and third-generation immigrants have adopted a religious identity? What does it offer them that other identities cannot satisfy?

2. How does Souad explain her decision to wear the veil? How did she expect others to respond? What responses did she get?

3. How do different people in this reading explain why women wear the veil?

4. In the West, many Muslim women choose to wear the veil. In Iran and some other Islamic states, the veil is mandatory. In your opinion, does it make a difference? Do all mandatory traditions or rituals assume that the person who practices them has no choice? Have you ever embraced or chosen a commonplace tradition in your community?

5. Why does Fariba feel that she is a "barometer for the popularity of Muslims"?

6. Fadela Amara believes that for many, the veil is a marker of identity, but she says that others wear the veil to express their militancy and to show support for Islamic extremism. In her writings she suggests that it is also a sign of male dominance over women—a symbol of a society that does not respect the equality of women. If she is correct, how should the French people and government respond?

[1] Tariq Ramadan, *To Be a European Muslim* (Leicester: The Islamic Foundation, 1999), 114–15.

[2] Quoted in John R. Bowen, *Why the French Don't Like Headscarves: Islam, the State, and Public Space* (Princeton: Princeton University Press, 2007), 76–77.

[3] Quoted in ibid., 79–80.

[4] Fadela Amara, *Breaking the Silence: French Women's Voices from the Ghetto*, trans. Helen Harden Chenut (Los Angeles: University of California Press, 2006), 73–74.

[5] Ibid., 74.

A Brief History of the Veil in Islam

"To this day, head coverings play a significant role in many religions, including Orthodox Judaism and Catholicism."

Scarves and veils of different colors and shapes were customary in countless cultures long before Islam came into being in the seventh century in the Arabian Peninsula (which includes present-day Saudi Arabia). To this day, head coverings play a significant role in many religions, including Orthodox Judaism and Catholicism. Since the seventh century, Islam has grown to be one of the major world religions.* As it spread through the Middle East to Saharan and sub-Saharan Africa, to Central Asia, and to many different societies around the Arabian Sea (see map on page 61), it incorporated some local veiling customs and influenced others. But it is only recently that some Islamic states, such as Iran, have begun to require all women to wear the veil (in Iran it is called the *chador*, which covers the entire body).

Critics of the Muslim veiling tradition argue that women do not wear the veil by choice, and they are often forced to cover their heads and bodies. In contrast, many daughters of Muslim immigrants in the West argue that the veil symbolizes devotion and piety and that veiling is their own choice. To them it is a question of religious identity and self-expression.

What are the origins of the obligation to wear the Islamic veil (or *hijab* in Arabic)? Do all Muslim women wear the veil? Do they have to? Also, are all veils the same, or do they take different forms and shapes? And, finally, what objections does the veil raise in some countries in the West? Sociologist Caitlin Killian explains that, in the past as in the present, the tradition of veiling has been influenced by different religious interpretations as well as by politics.

> Muslim religious writings are not entirely clear on the question of women veiling. Various statements in the Quran and the Hadith (statements attributed to the prophet Mohammed) make reference to Mohammed's wives veiling, but it is debatable whether these statements apply only to the Prophet's wives or to all Muslim women. While the need for women to be modest is mentioned, the area women must cover depends on the source and ranges from "the bosom" to the whole body except the face and hands. The veil is a vehicle for distinguishing between women and men and a means of controlling male sexual desire. . . . Muslim men are also urged to be modest and to cover themselves between the waist and the knees. . . . [In some Islamic societies] an immodest woman brings dishonor not only on herself but also on her male family members. . . . The veil itself, however, predated Islam and was practiced by women of several religions. It also was largely linked to class position: Wealthy women could

---

* Islam began as a small faith community in the Arabian Peninsula. The community was established in Medina by the prophet Mohammed (c. 570–632 CE). From there it spread through the Middle East to Saharan and sub-Saharan Africa, to Central Asia, and to many societies around the Arabian Sea. After Islam was established in the Middle East and North Africa, it made significant inroads into Europe, as well.

The *hijab* is one name for a variety of similar headscarves. It is the most popular veil worn in the West. These veils consist of one or two scarves that cover the head and neck. Outside the West, this traditional veil is worn by many Muslim women in the Arab world and beyond.

The *niqab* covers the entire body, head and face; however, an opening is left for the eyes. The two main styles of *niqab* are the half-*niqab* that consists of a headscarf and facial veil that leaves the eyes and part of the forehead visible and the full, or Gulf, *niqab* that leaves only a narrow slit for the eyes. Although these veils are popular across the Muslim world, they are most common in the Gulf States. The *niqab* is responsible for creating much debate within Europe. Some politicians have argued for its ban, while others feel that it interferes with communication or creates security concerns.

The *chador* is a full-body-length shawl held closed at the neck by hand or pin. It covers the head and the body but leaves the face completely visible. *Chadors* are most often black and are most common in the Middle East, specifically in Iran.

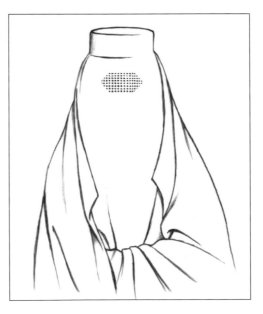

The *burqa* is a full-body veil. The wearer's entire face and body are covered, and one sees through a mesh screen over the eyes. It is most commonly worn in Afghanistan and Pakistan. Under the Taliban regime in Afghanistan (1996–2001), its use was mandated by law.

afford to veil their bodies completely, whereas poor women who had to work [in the field] either modified their veils or did not wear them at all.

The numerous styles of Islamic dress throughout the world today reflect local traditions and different interpretations of Islamic requirements. Muslim women in France, therefore, exhibit a wide range of dress and head coverings. Many wear nothing that distinguishes them as Muslims. A number of immigrant women practice modesty, not by donning traditional dress (i.e., the North African *djellaba*), but rather by wearing long-sleeved shirts and skirts that reach the ankles. For those who do veil, some simply wear brightly colored scarves on their heads, sometimes even allowing hair to show; others pin unicolor veils tightly around the face; and still others adopt long, flowing Islamic dress and occasionally cover the entire face except for the eyes. The girls at the center of the controversy usually wear Western clothing with a veil pinned around the face to cover their hair.

The struggle over Maghrebian women's dress began long before their immigration to France in the 1970s. French and British colonizers encouraged Muslim women to remove the veil and emulate European women. Consequently, in Algeria and other North African and Middle Eastern countries, the veil became a symbol of national identity and opposition to the West during independence and nationalist movements.[1]

Connections

1. What religious or cultural symbols are important to you or your family? How important do you think they are for others? How would you feel if people pressured you not to display them?

2. How do you explain the fact that there are so many different interpretations of whether or not Muslims choose to wear the veil?

3. Why has the veil become such an important symbol and thus the focus of controversy? What everyday objects in your life have become political symbols? Why? What do you think the veil represents in the eyes of non-Muslims?

4. When do clothes become political? Why did the veil become a political symbol for Muslims who fought against European colonialism? How do people in your community use clothes to express their political views and identities?

[1] We removed all citations from this excerpt. For the full text, see Caitlin Killian, "The Other Side of the Veil: North African Women in France Respond to the Headscarf Affair," *Gender and Society*, 17, no. 4 (August 2003): 569–70.

Public Schools:
Where New Citizens Are Made

"The challenge facing the inclusive school is therefore not to oppose cultures and traditions, but to start from the principle that each culture contributes a part of the whole . . . in order to forge a common feeling of belonging that does not deny the diversity of identities." – *Jean-Louis Auduc*

In the school setting, children of immigrants meet other French students and are introduced to the democratic principles of secular France: the ideas that all citizens have equal rights and that France maintains a separation between church and state so that people are free to choose their beliefs without interference. The secular nature of school is believed to be central to the proper integration of France's future citizens, and many in France believe that the success of this process depends on the neutrality (or, in this case, non-religious climate) of schools; religion, in short, has no room in public education.

In 2003, two girls were expelled from this multiethnic school in Aubervilliers, France, for wearing the veil.

The exclusion of religion from schools dates back to the late-eighteenth-century intellectual movement known as the Enlightenment and to the French Revolution that began in 1789. In reality, however, the separation of church and state was made into law only in 1905. But the Enlightenment view that students must be protected from ideological influences that may distort the truth continues to influence discussion about education to this day. The principles of *laïcité* (secularity) in schools, writes scholar Joan Wallach Scott, "dated to the . . . [Jules] Ferry laws (1881–82, 1886), which made primary education a requirement for boys and girls and which effectively banished from the classroom religion as a subject and priests and nuns as teachers."[1] Before the Ferry laws, education in France was dominated by the Catholic Church. From the perspective of Jules Ferry, Minister of Education at the time these laws were passed,

> [T]he school was to be the agent of assimilation; the goal of its pedagogy was to instill a common republican political identity in children from a diversity of backgrounds. The school was to effect a transition from private to public, from the world of the locality and the family to that of the nation. Teachers were the crucial element in this process—secular missionaries, charged with converting their pupils to the wonders of science and reason. . . . A shared language, culture, and ideological formation—and so a nation one and indivisible—was to be the *outcome* of the educational process. Schools were instruments for constructing the nation . . . the privileged site where differences were contained and transformed into Frenchness.[2]

In the eyes of most French, schools continue to be the place where future French citizens are made. In the mid-1990s, when passionate debates about headscarves filled the airwaves, the Ferry assimilation model was routinely invoked. Although this time the target was no longer the Catholic Church—it was the immigrants from Muslim countries—the rhetoric remained similar. In 1994, Education Minister François Bayrou issued a memorandum distinguishing between "discreet" symbols, which could be tolerated in public schools, and "ostentatious" symbols, including the Islamic veils, which were to be banned (this memo foreshadowed the ban of 2003). Defending French secularity, Bayrou argued that in France,

> . . . the national and republican projects have been identified with a certain idea of citizenship. This French idea of the nation and republic by nature respects all convictions, particularly religious and political beliefs and cultural traditions. But it rules out the breaking down of the nation into separate communities which are indifferent to one another, and which respect only their own rules and laws and only engage in a simple coexistence. The nation is not only a group of citizens who hold individual rights. It is a community with a [common] destiny. This ideal is constructed firstly at school. School is the space which more than any other involves education and integration where all children and all youth are to be found, learning to live together and respect one another. . . . This secular and national ideal is the very substance of the republican school and the foundation of its duty of civic education.[3]

More than 200 years after the Revolution, France is facing new challenges around the issue of religion. In addition to the tensions surrounding the Muslim immigrants and their sons and daughters, schools also face tensions between different minorities. A great number of people in France now believe that religion is threatening the mission of educating new French citizens. Although public schools suffer from a lack of resources, teacher shortages, and violence, many teachers continue to believe that religious tensions are the source of the problem and argue that the cultivation of a "common culture" is their most important challenge. In a number of testimonies, American scholar Trica Keaton had teachers report on their classroom experience. One literature teacher explained:

> We are told we are supposed to take children and turn them into citizens. The school is there to make you a citizen, to make you French, which means speaking the language and knowing [traditional] French culture. This is what we try to convey through education.[4]

Resisting the idea of "multiculturalism" (which many in France feel threatens community cohesion), the French school curriculum focuses on the values associated with the "Republic": secularism and the concepts of liberty, equality, and brotherhood (in French, *liberté, égalité, fraternité*—principles that originated in the French Revolution). Schools also highlight French literature and history, with the idea of promoting a "common culture" among their students. A history professor shared his thoughts on this issue:

> I ask myself, is a common culture . . . transmitted . . . by the school and by national education . . . deculturing [taking cultural identity away from] those who have their own culture? Personally, I think the answer is yes. . . . I believe with all my heart that it's a good thing. It's good because I am profoundly republican and *laïque* (secular), through my education, through the way I function as a citizen and as a human being. . . . I think that our society has arrived at a point where it seems that our standards for a common culture, so that they harmonize, must go through a de-Christianization, a de-Islamization, among other things. I mean that the deculturation, or acculturation [training people in a common culture] . . . can lead to that common cement that binds us.[5]

An increasing number of educators see the schools' mission in a different light. They emphasize the importance of teaching mutual respect between mainstream culture and minority culture. They also criticize those parts of the public schools' curriculum that ignore the painful period when France colonized countries in Africa and Asia. Jean-Louis Auduc, assistant director of the Institut Universitaire de Formation des Maîtres de Créteil (a teacher training institute), argues that educating new citizens "must . . . be based on those non-negotiable values which are the basis for a social democracy: rejection of racism or sexism, respect for human rights."[6] He explains:

> Schools must be places of understanding, of knowledge of other cultures, especially to bring their pupils to understand the part each culture occupies in the whole. . . . The struggle against racism, anti-Semitism, discriminatory practices is everybody's business, not just the business of the individual communities concerned. . . . The challenge facing the inclusive school is therefore not to oppose cultures and traditions, but to start from the principle that each culture contributes a part of the whole . . . in order to forge a common feeling of belonging that does not deny the diversity of identities.[7]

Connections

1. What was the role of public education, according to nineteenth-century Education Minister Jules Ferry? What do you see as the role of education in a multiethnic, multireligious society?

2. Why did Education Minister François Bayrou think, in 1994, that education should be protected from the influence of religion?

3. Teachers in France are required to educate new citizens. What do you think this means? What values are they expected to teach their students? Is that the role of teachers in your society?

4. One of the teachers seems to imply that he believes a common culture can only exist in a society without religion. Do you agree with this position?

5. At the heart of the debate about France's "common culture" lies the question of language. French identity (and this is true for other countries, as well) is linked to a standard, or official, language. As one teacher reported, teachers in immigrant neighborhoods are keen to make their students aware of the disadvantages of using slang:

   > These are students from Seine-Saint-Denis.[*] . . . [I]t means that they are students who have their own language, the language of the *cité* [housing project]. So my role is to make them understand that there is a place where you can speak like that and other places where you must not speak like that, where you cannot. I have to show them continually that they can express themselves, but that they don't have to be taken for a fool, if they speak normally not like they do in the *cité*. . . . So I have to make them understand that they are not going to find a job if they continue to speak like that. You **see**, it's not only a question of vocabulary, if you will, it's also a question of attitude, clothing, the way they dress.[8]

   How important is it to learn the language, customs, and ideas that are used by mainstream society? Does adopting the dress, language, and culture of the mainstream make you a "sellout"?

6. According to Auduc's philosophy, how would teachers prepare for their duties? Why might some people resist Auduc's ideas?

---

[*] Seine-Saint-Denis is an administrative department of France, northeast of Paris, often called simply "the 93" (*le neuf trois*), a reference to its administrative number. In recent decades it has been populated by many immigrants, much like other suburbs (*banlieues*) on the outskirts of Paris and other metropolitan areas. The 2005 riots that started in Clichy-sous-Bois—one of the communes that make up Seine-Saint-Denis—indicate some of the social and ethnic tensions in the district.

[1] Joan Wallach Scott, *The Politics of the Veil* (Princeton: Princeton University Press, 2007), 99.

[2] Scott, *The Politics of the Veil*, 98–99.

[3] François Bayrou, as quoted by Meira Levinson, "Liberalism Versus Democracy? Schooling Private Citizens in the Public Square," *British Journal of Political Science* 27 (1997): 352. We thank Levinson for her help with these readings.

[4] Trica Danielle Keaton, *Muslim Girls and the Other France: Race, Identity Politics, and Social Exclusion* (Bloomington: Indiana University Press, 2006), 92.

[5] Quoted in Keaton, *Muslim Girls and the Other France*, 103.

[6] Jean-Louis Auduc, "Forging a Common Sense of Belonging: Respecting the Diversity of Identities," *Prospects* 36, no. 3 (September 2006): 322.

[7] Ibid., 323, 326.

[8] Quoted in Keaton, *Muslim Girls and the Other France*, 109.

The Veil at School

"[I]n educational institutions, students' wearing of symbols that indicate their religious beliefs is not in itself incompatible with the principle of [secularity], to the extent that the wearing of such symbols constitutes the exercise of freedom of expression and freedom to express religious beliefs." — *Le Conseil d'État, 1989*

At the beginning of the 1989 school year, the Gabriel-Havez Middle School in the town of Creil was abuzz. At the center of all the commotion were three young girls who decided to wear Muslim headscarves to school. Teachers felt that this was a distraction, if not a violation, of France's tradition of excluding religion from public schools. For years Muslim veils had been a daily sight. But now they stirred up anxiety and anger as the mood in the country turned against this widespread Muslim custom.

The three girls—15-year-old Samira Saidani and two sisters, 14-year-old Leila and 13-year-old Fatima Achaboun—went to school with other children whose parents came mostly from France's former North African colonies: Tunisia, Morocco, and Algeria (collectively known as the Maghreb). When the girls refused the principal's demand that they remove their headscarves, they were sent home. Later, after several rounds of negotiations between school administrators, the parents, and local organizations, a compromise was reached: the girls could wear their headscarves in school but had to drop them down to their shoulders in class.[1] The agreement held for a few days, but when the three again started to wear the scarves in class, a new round of negotiations began—this time at a national level. Catholic, Muslim, and Jewish organizations joined the discussion, as did the media, which did much to draw public attention to this local story and to tie it to questions of democracy, secularity, and women's rights. Politicians, political analysts, and public intellectuals all added their opinions, and this local event became the first "veil affair" (*l'affaire du foulard*).

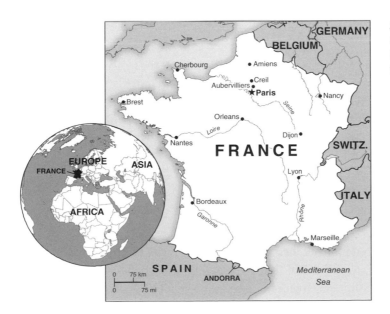

A map of France including Creil and Aubervilliers, the suburbs of Paris where the headscarf affair took place

Fatima Achaboun, a young Tunisian girl, is shown surrounded by friends in 1989 in the school courtyard after the school authorized her return on the condition that she did not wear her veil in the classroom.

Luis Cardoso, a history and geography teacher at the Gabriel-Havez Middle School, followed the event from the beginning. In an interview, Cardoso argued that "though the headscarf need not be condemned, it is nevertheless capable of generating conflict of moderate or long duration in [poor] neighborhoods where the problems are already numerous and often exacerbated."[2] But he continued,

> The debate about religion and public school is just one of many problems we must face on an everyday basis. These problems, which take a toll on the students, are domestic, social, and racial; delinquency and violence also play large roles. In this climate, the children of North African origin do not pose any more problems than do the other kids. To suggest the opposite seems false to me, as does the suggestion that the majority of them are failing out of school. . . . [But those] who think that the issues are simple and straightforward and that everyone should just be allowed to do as they please, to be exempt from all rules, should come and spend a little time in Creil and rub up [against] the reality of the situation.[3]

Cardoso and many other teachers felt that the best way to allow them to focus on the real issues at school—those that Cardoso mentioned in the excerpt above—was to ban the veil. Commentators from across the political spectrum joined the opposition to the scarves, and many argued that the 1989 "veil affair" demonstrated that "it is impossible for Muslims to assimilate universal values and/or integrate into French society."[4]

The Gabriel-Havez Middle School case was finally referred to the Conseil d'État, the highest administrative court in France. The Conseil surprised many when it ruled that in educational institutions,

> [S]tudents' wearing of symbols that indicate their religious beliefs is not in itself incompatible with the principle of [secularity], to the extent that the wearing of such symbols constitutes the exercise of freedom of expression and freedom to express religious beliefs. Such freedom

> does not, however, extend to permitting students to wear religious symbols that . . . would constitute an act of pressure, provocation, proselytism or propaganda, or detract from the dignity or freedom of the student or other members of the educational community . . . or disrupt the establishment or normal operation of the public service [translation].[5]

The ruling was reversed in 2003, but for 14 years, France's highest administrative court did not think that the Muslim veil (or other religious symbols) necessarily conflicted with the idea of secularity.

Connections

1. Luis Cardoso explained that headscarves "generate conflict" in schools. What kinds of symbols and clothes can generate conflict in your school? What do teachers do about them? What kind of response is appropriate to such conflicts in schools? When do they become an educational opportunity? A distraction?

2. Why do you think many people in France began to object to girls wearing headscarves in schools?

3. Is it right for teachers and school administrators to tell their students what to wear to school? When do teachers' interventions infringe on the students' right to self-expression?

4. What reasons did the Conseil d'État give for allowing headscarves in public schools? Do you agree or disagree with this decision?

---

[1] Robert Carle, "*Hijab* and the Limits of French Secular Republicanism," *Society*, 41 no. 6 (September 2004): 64.

[2] Luis Cardoso, "At the Heart of the 'Affair': A Professor from Creil Provides Testimony," *The Veil*, University of North Carolina at Chapel Hill website, *http://www.unc.edu/depts/europe/conferences/Veil2000/articles/translations/Cardoso.doc* (accessed January 9, 2008).

[3] Ibid.

[4] Riva Kastoryano, "France's Veil Affair," *Inroads* 15 (Summer/Fall 2004): *http://www.findarticles.com/p/articles/mi_qa4014/is_200407/ai_n9467219* (accessed January 25, 2007). We thank Kastoryano for her help and advice. The opposition to the veil was very broad: a large segment of the French public claimed that Islam (or any religion, for that matter) split the country along sectarian or ethnic lines (the French use the pejorative term *communautarisme*). And while the Left claimed that Islam may prove to be incompatible with Western liberal values, the far Right argued that the Muslim population was undercutting France's historical Christian identity. Even traditionally progressive groups argued against the veil: some feminists, for example, claimed that the veil symbolized women's oppression in this community. See Norma Moruzzi, "A Problem with Headscarves," 659–64. For the feminist perspective, see Fadéla Amara, *Breaking the Silence: French Women's Voices from the Ghetto*, trans. Helen Harden Chenut (Los Angeles: University of California Press, 2006), 98–102.

[5] Quoted in Library of Parliament, "Freedom of Religion and Religious Symbols in the Public Sphere," Parliament of Canada website, *http://www.parl.gc.ca/information/library/PRBpubs/prb0441-e.pdf* (accessed November 26, 2007).

The Integration of Jews in Modern France

"We must refuse everything to the Jews as a nation and accord everything to the Jew as an individual." – French Deputy Clermont-Tonnerre (1789)

Shortly after the French Revolution broke out in the spring of 1789, a new body called the National Constituent Assembly was formed with the goals of leading radical reforms of the French government and of rewriting the French constitution. In August of 1789, it took a major step toward the upending of the monarchy: it adopted The Declaration of the Rights of Man and Citizen, a political document that begins with the words, "Men are born and remain free and equal in rights."[1] Thus, in its first sentence, the Declaration states that all Frenchmen are entitled to a defined set of natural, universal rights.

The French Declaration addressed individual rights, and it was designed to open up the political and economic system to all citizens. Fulfilling its commitment to the revolutionary principle of equal rights to all, in 1791 France gave full rights to its Jews—its largest non-Christian minority. Thus, the Jews of France were the first European Jews to receive full "emancipation." Their rights, however, came with a provision. As a French deputy named Clermont-Tonnerre put it, "We must refuse everything to the Jews as a nation and accord everything to the Jew as an individual."[2] In other words, as long as Jews kept their collective identity and religious practice private, their rights as French citizens were ensured. But the constitution granted nothing to them as a minority group (to this day the term "minority"—*minorité*—is regarded as divisive in France). The Jews by and large accepted this model of citizenship, which required cultural assimilation as a precondition for full civil liberties.

In 1799, ten years after the Revolution began, Napoleon Bonaparte overturned the first French Republic by declaring himself emperor. The Republic was no more, but questions of French citizenship and nationality still haunted the French: many of them feared and even resented the presence of religious minorities among them. In 1807, less than twenty years after Jewish emancipation, Napoleon approached a group of French Jewish religious leaders in order to find out how loyal they were. He asked,

> In the eyes of the Jews, are Frenchmen considered as their brethren? Or are they considered as strangers?
>
> Do Jews born in France, and treated by the laws as French citizens, consider France their country? Are they bound to defend it? Are they bound to obey the laws and to conform to the dispositions of the civil code?[3]

Since the Jews had been living in France since the beginning of the Common Era, the fact that in 1807 Napoleon questioned their loyalty is telling. It reveals the ambiguity many French felt toward the religious and national identities of minority groups; for many of them, non-Catholics living in France were lesser French who were not to be trusted. Fully aware of these assumptions, the Jews at the meeting pledged their undivided allegiance to France:

> The love of country is in the heart of Jews a sentiment so natural, so powerful, and so consonant to their religious opinions, that a French Jew considers himself in England as among strangers, although he may be among Jews; and the case is the same with English Jews in France.
>
> To such a pitch is this sentiment carried among them, that during the last war, French Jews have been seen fighting desperately against other Jews, the subjects of countries then at war with France.[4]

The Jewish leaders stated clearly that their allegiance was to France and that their religious affiliation was secondary to their national identity.

In the decades following this exchange, Jews climbed slowly but steadily up the social ladder in France. Many of them made names for themselves as artists, authors, and scientists; others developed flourishing businesses; still others enjoyed successful careers in politics and in the military. But an upsurge of antisemitism toward the end of the century disrupted their progress. Tensions finally erupted in 1894, when Captain Alfred Dreyfus, a high-ranking Jewish officer in the French army, was falsely charged with treason, convicted, and sent to prison on Devil's Island. "The Dreyfus Affair," as it came to be called, revealed deep-seated resentment toward Jews. But Dreyfus also had several high-profile supporters. Among them was the author Émile Zola, who published a famous 1898 letter entitled J'accuse! (I Accuse!). In it, Zola accused the French Army of antisemitism and a miscarriage of justice. In an earlier writing entitled "A Plea for the Jews," Zola passionately exposed the flagrant antisemitism of nineteenth-century France. He wrote:

> For several years, with growing surprise and disgust, I have been following the campaign that people in France are trying to mount against the Jews. It seems to me a monstrosity: by that I mean something that is altogether beyond the bounds of common sense, truth and justice, a blind and stupid thing that would drag us back centuries in time, ultimately a thing that would lead to religious persecution, which is the worst of abominations and would bathe every country in blood.
>
> And I am determined to say this. First of all, what are the Jews accused of? What are they reproached with?
>
> Some people, even friends of mine, say that they cannot bear them, that they cannot touch their hands without their skin crawling with revulsion. It is a matter of physical horror, the repulsion of one race for another, of the white man for the yellow man, of the red man for the black man. I do not ask whether part of this revulsion doesn't stem from the ancient anger of the Christian against the Jew . . .

But if the truth be told, that reason—the hostility of one race towards another—is not sufficient. We might as well revert to the depths of the forest: we might as well recommence the barbarous war that pits one species against another; we might as well devour one another because we do not utter the same cries and our fur does not grow in the same way. What civilizations strive for is precisely to erase that savage need to hurl ourselves at our fellow creature, when he does not resemble us exactly. . . .

Now I come to the real reproach, the serious one, which is essentially a social matter. I shall merely sum up the arguments of the prosecution, merely outline them. The Jews are accused of being a nation within the nation, of separately leading the life of a religious caste and thus of transcending borders, of being a sort of international sect which has no real mother country and which, if it were to triumph one day, would be capable of dominating the world . . .

But while we may observe the fact, we must also explain it. What we must add is that the Jews, as they exist today, are our creation, the result of eighteen hundred years of idiotic persecution. Since we have penned them up in revolting districts like so many lepers, it is not in the least surprising if they have lived apart, preserved all of their traditions and tightened the family bonds, remaining the vanquished among the victors. Since we have struck them and insulted them and heaped injustice and violence upon them, it is not in the least surprising if deep down in their hearts, even unconsciously, they nurture the hope of revenge in some distant future, the will to resist, to stay alive and to vanquish.[5]

Zola's letter highlighted the brutality implicit in racial discrimination. Zola's warning remains particularly haunting, because it aptly describes prejudices that persisted well into the twentieth century. Indeed, it points out sentiments that led to the targeting of French Jews during War World II. The Vichy government, which collaborated with the Nazis during the war, enacted discriminatory laws against the Jews of France and sent many of them to internment camps. From these camps the Vichy government deported more than 75,000 of an estimated 300,000 French Jews to Nazi death camps, where most of them were murdered.

Instances of antisemitism in the French capital came to a head in 2006 with the racially motivated kidnapping, torture, and murder of 26-year-old French Jew Ilan Halimi. He was lured into a trap by a woman and then held for ransom by a gang of Muslim youths from the Paris suburbs until his death. The horrific event sparked outrage across the country and led to cross-cultural condemnation of racism. Here, two members of the Paris Sikh community participate in one of the demonstrations. The headline in the *Jewish News* reads, "Our assassinated child."

Unfortunately, in the aftermath of the Holocaust, the French government was reluctant to acknowledge the extent of local collaboration with the Vichy regime and its role in the Holocaust. Since the 1960s, however, antisemitism in France has been in decline, and many Jews have made the Republic their home.[6] Moreover, since the mid-1990s, many in France have begun to speak of the Judeo-Christian civilization, highlighting ancient cultural ties.

At the same time, since the late 1980s, a new form of antisemitism emerged. In contrast to the "old" one, the new antisemitism is often associated with the conflict between Israel and the Palestinians. While some in France simply criticize Israel for its treatment of the Palestinians, others—and among them are young French Muslims—use the conflict to promote hatred against Jews in general. Economics and social status also play a role in the dynamic between the two communities (much like the majority of the Muslims in France, the majority of the 600,000 French Jews originated from North Africa). The relative success of the French Jews (real and imagined) is used to promote hatred against all Jews, hatred that often draws on old stereotypes of the Jew as all-powerful, deceitful, and unduly rich.[7] The antisemitic incidents in the late 1990s and early 2000s were later used by proponents of the ban on veils in public schools where religious and ethnic tensions were felt acutely.[8] Proponents argue that such a ban will help curb Islamic radicalization. These supporters of the ban believe that France needs to return to its assimilation model and that, to ensure the peace of the entire community, religion must be kept private.

Connections

1. What formula did the French adopt during the French Revolution to assign rights to Jews and other minorities? Why do you think they chose this policy? How does this policy compare with the way in which the issue of rights for religious minorities is addressed in the United States today?

2. What did Napoleon try to find out about the Jews in France? What was his concern? How did they respond to him questioning their loyalty? Do you think that ethnic and national identities are compatible? Why?

3. What, according to Zola, were the prejudices and stereotypes that contributed to the charges Dreyfus faced?

4. Who, according to Zola, is responsible for the state of affairs in which the Jews found themselves at the end of the nineteenth century? How does Zola explain the anger in the Jewish community?

5. Some critics argue that there is a close resemblance between the traditional French antisemitism and the anti-Muslim sentiments in contemporary France. Is it a fair comparison? Why or why not?

6. Scholars Jonathan Laurence and Justine Vaisse write about antisemitism in French schools. They describe a dilemma many teachers in France face:

> Antiracism associations have argued that there is an educational mission to fulfill among the younger generations, whether Muslim, Jewish, or nonminority, and that the trick is to make them more sensitive to the issue of anti-Semitism and racism without stigmatizing a whole community.[9]

What is the dilemma educators face when they seek to address antisemitism in school?

Excerpted from Emile Zola's letter, *J'accuse*, published on January 13, 1898 in *L'Aurore*.

---

[1] French National Assembly, "Declaration of the Rights of Man and Citizen," *http://www.yale.edu/lawweb/avalon/rightsof.htm*.

[2] Count Stanislas-Marie-Adelaide de Clermont-Tonnerre, "Speech on Religious Minorities and Questionable Professions," December 23, 1789, Center for History and New Media website, *http://chnm.gmu.edu/revolution/d/284/* (accessed on June 13, 2008).

[3] Facing History and Ourselves, *Holocaust and Human Behavior* (Brookline: Facing History and Ourselves National Foundation, 1994), 80.

[4] Ibid., 80.

[5] Émile Zola, *The Dreyfus Affair: J'accuse and Other Writings*, ed. Alain Pagès, trans. Eleanor Levieux (New Haven: Yale University Press, 1996), 2–3.

[6] Jean-Marc Dreyfus and Jonathan Laurence, "Anti-Semitism in France," *US-France Analysis Brief*, Center on the U.S. and France, Brookings Institution website (May 2002), *http://www.bc.edu/schools/cas/polisci/meta-elements/pdf/laurence.pdf* (accessed September 4, 2008).

[7] Henri Hajdenberg, a former president of the France's largest umbrella organization of Jewish groups, the Representative Council of Jewish Institutions, explained in 2006: "The anti-Semitism being felt in France may be ideologically rooted in anger against Israel, but it is fed by a new generation also taking up old anti-Semitic delusions—that all Jews are rich, that all Jews are powerful, that Jews are to blame for all the poverty and problems faced in immigrant communities." See Colin Nickerson, "Anti-Semitism seen Rising among France's Muslims," The *Boston Globe* website, March 13, 2006, *http://www.boston.com/news/world/europe/articles/2006/03/13/anti_semitism_seen_rising_among_frances_muslims/* (accessed September 4, 2008).

[8] Jonathan Laurence and Justin Vaisse, *Integrating Islam: Political and Religious Challenges in Contemporary France* (Washington: The Brookings Institute, 2006), 238–39.

[9] Ibid., 239–40.

Debating the Ban of the Veil in Public Schools

"The girls who veil in France, especially the high school and junior high students, it's first of all a question of identity, because these girls are born in France to foreign parents." — Isma, 36-year-old Algerian teacher

French citizens found themselves grappling with a number of pressing issues at the beginning of the new millennium. In predominantly French-Maghrebian neighborhoods, social unrest relating to poverty and discrimination was on the rise, compounding ethnic conflicts stemming from the real and imaginary differences between these North African French and the European French. Meanwhile, religious tensions surrounding the presence of a large Muslim population in a secular state flared, intensified by growing fears of Islamic radicalism following 9/11 and other terrorist attacks in Europe.

These tensions were especially sharp in public schools that had large numbers of Muslim students, and they soon seemed to focus on the Islamic veil. In 2004, roughly 70 percent of the nation felt that the veil was an obstacle to France's national unity, to its secular and democratic tradition, and to its security. Both Left and Right agreed: the veil had to be banned in public schools.

The year before, President Jacques Chirac had called on Bernard Stasi, a former minister, to head a commission to study the veil and other aspects of Muslim life that affected France's secular tradition. Lawmakers, school administrators, and the general public expected drastic actions. However, little attention was paid to the question of why Muslim girls and women were wearing the veil. Sociologist Caitlin Killian attempted to answer this question. During the debate, she interviewed female Muslim immigrants

While there are many state-funded Jewish and Catholic schools in France, there are only a handful of Muslim schools funded by the state.

about a range of related issues including racism, assimilation, school curriculums, and teachers' attitudes toward the veil (or, in the case of men, the beards some Muslims wear). The findings pointed to a broad spectrum of opinions regarding all of these issues. Focusing on the veil, Killian found, on the one hand, women who vigorously defended its ban in schools and, on the other, women who thought that the veil was a legitimate form of self-expression.

Some of the women Killian interviewed argued that there are much more urgent issues at school than the wearing of the veil (violence and poor behavior among them). According to others, the French are specifically targeting Muslim culture. They also thought that the proposed ban on headscarves in schools is driven by prejudice. Yusra, a 31-year-old Moroccan, explained:

> I find that it's really an attitude on the part of teachers that is really racist, truly. That, for me, is a racist act. We cannot exclude girls because they wear the headscarf. . . . It's really pointing a finger at them, and then [at] the culture of the child, they say to her "your culture, it's not good." You don't have a right to judge like that.[1]

While some of the interviewees viewed the French reaction to the headscarf affair as racist, others questioned the secularity of schools where most of the holidays and vacations revolved around the Catholic calendar.[2] Some went on to suggest that instead of ignoring or banning Islamic traditions, teachers could use them to educate about the cultural and religious diversity of France's students. Below are a few women's reflections:

> **Besma, a 34-year-old Tunisian:** I'm going to repeat what a lot of Arabs say, there are schools in France, or universities in France, where there are no exams on Saturday because it's the [Jewish] Sabbath, in the public schools, in the secular schools, and nobody talks about it. All that it takes is for the universities to agree. . . . The students manage to make an [informal] arrangement with the teachers. . . . On Friday, they eat a lean meal, meaning a meatless meal because Catholics don't eat meat on Friday. We do Lent Friday in school cafeterias, and nobody protests. Nobody finds anything to say. So I find it completely petty to hide behind arguments that don't hold up, that aren't at all convincing, and all of sudden there are different rules for different groups.

> **Nour, a 34-year-old Algerian:** [Y]ou know the secular school, it doesn't miss celebrating Easter, and when they celebrate Easter, it doesn't bother me. My daughter comes home with painted Easter eggs and everything; it's pretty; it's cute. There are classes that are over 80 percent Maghrebian in the suburbs, and they celebrate Easter, they celebrate Christmas, you see? And that's not a problem for the secular school. And I don't find that fair. . . . I find that when it's Ramadan, they should talk about Ramadan. Honestly, me, it wouldn't be a problem. On the contrary, someone who comes into class . . . with a veil, that would pose a question actually, that we could discuss in class, to know why this person wears the veil. . . . Why is it so upsetting to have someone in class who wears a veil, when we could make it a subject of discussion on all religions? Getting stuck on the veil hides the question. They make such a big deal out of

it, the poor girls, they take them out of school; people turn them into extraterrestrials. In the end we turn them into people who will have problems in their identities, in their culture and everything. . . . For a country that is home to so many cultures, there's no excuse.[3]

Some of the women Killian interviewed argued that the veil is a symbol of a new identity, especially for the second-generation immigrants who experience rejection in their daily life in France. The veil, they suggested, is the response of those who seek alternatives to the French national identity. Isma, a 36-year-old Algerian teacher who now teaches in France, had this to say:

The girls who veil in France, especially the high school and junior high students, it's first of all a question of identity, because these girls are born in France to foreign parents. . . . At a given time an adolescent wants to affirm himself, to show that he's someone, that he's an individual, so he thinks, I'd say, he thinks that it's by his clothes that he shows that he comes from somewhere [else], that he's someone [different]. So then, I think you should let them do it, and afterwards, by themselves, people come back to who they really are.[4]

But other female immigrants argued that Muslims girls should assimilate or keep their traditions to themselves. Some felt that the veil promotes fundamentalism and intolerance, while others still saw it as a sign of female oppression:

Cherifa, a 44-year-old Moroccan: I believe that if they have to wear the veil then they should do it at home. Me, I'd be a bit radical. I wouldn't make concessions, because if I want to wear a *djellaba* [Middle Eastern cloak] . . . then I should stay in my country. I feel that when you are somewhere, you try to blend in. There's an old Moroccan proverb that says "do as your neighbor [does] or leave." That means that I shouldn't come to France to affirm my convictions, be they cultural or religious and all. If I want to wear *babouches* [Moroccan slippers] and put on the veil . . . well I should stay in my country, or I blend in. Otherwise, if I'm in France, well I'm sorry, I dress like the French. If I eat with them, live with them, if I go to their schools, I don't see why I'd make myself be noticed because I want to wear, um, they should wear it when they're at home or at friends. I don't have anything against it. But when she's at school and everything, I don't think so. . . . No, I would totally agree with them outlawing the veil.[5]

Deha, a 34-year-old Algerian: I come from a school [in Algeria] where the veil was already starting. It's not the way she dresses; it's what she is herself. The way she dresses implies a lot of things; so there are no sports, philosophy is forbidden. . . . A girl who wears the veil [thinks that] she's pure and that the other who doesn't wear the veil, she's not pure. It's not that she's not pure; it's that she's a slut. You see? And it's there that you say to yourself, well, okay, the veil represents all of that.

Isma, a 36-year-old Algerian: I'm not intolerant; myself, I've suffered from intolerance, but dressing like that, you become yourself intolerant, because you want to impose. I'm sorry to say it, but it's often the one who wants to show that he's more Muslim than the other; he wants to impose it.[6]

Connections

1. What ideas do you hear in the interviews regarding the veil, assimilation, and integration? What explanations did the women Killian interviewed offer for why some Muslim girls wear the veil? What accounts for the differences in their opinions?

2. What did the majority of the French public think about the girls who wear the veil? Do you think the veil is an obstacle to integration?

3. In her interview, Nour said that discussing issues such as the veil creates an educational opportunity. What does she think students could gain from these conversations? What is lost when such issues are ignored? How do you create a classroom that allows for those kinds of frank discussions?

4. What do clothes say about the people who wear them? When do they become an expression of identity? Can the clothes we wear transform us?

5. Do you think that forcing veiled Muslim girls to take off the veil in the classroom infringes on their religious rights? In the last excerpt, Nour seems to claim that it can breed hatred. What do you think?

6. During the civil rights movement in the United States, some African Americans wore a hairstyle called the Afro, which was considered an expression of black history, culture, and pride. When do expressions of identity become a protest?

---

[1] Quoted in Caitlin Killian, "The Other Side of the Veil: North African Women in France Respond to the Headscarf Affair," *Gender and Society*, 17, no. 4 (August 2003): 577.

[2] Killian, "The Other Side of the Veil," 577.

[3] Ibid., 578.

[4] Ibid., 579.

[5] Ibid., 582.

[6] Ibid., 583.

France Bans the Veil in Public Schools

"Secularism guarantees freedom of conscience. It protects the freedom to believe or not to believe." – Jacques Chirac, 2003

When the Stasi Commission completed its survey, it recommended a series of actions to combat the social and religious tensions in the suburbs, including adding Jewish and Muslim religious holidays to the school calendar and emphasizing teaching about religion, slavery, and decolonization in North Africa. Other proposals included measures to improve life in immigrant neighborhoods and the implementation of a newly created charter of *laïcité* to be recited at naturalization ceremonies for new citizens.[1]

Among the Commission's recommendations was also a proposal to ban the veil in public schools, a measure that many felt should be central to a new law aimed at defending France's secularity. President Chirac defended the proposal to ban the veil and other large religious symbols in schools. This was the only recommendation that the French legislature ended up adopting.

This was the right decision, Chirac argued, because the veil was an "aggressive" symbol and France could no longer accept "ostentatious signs of religious proselytism [trying to persuade people to follow a particular religion]."[2] In a nationally televised speech, Chirac also defended his vision of a unified, secular France:

> Splitting society into communities cannot be the choice for France. It would be contrary to our history, traditions and culture. . . . Secularism guarantees freedom of conscience. It protects the freedom to believe or not to believe. It guarantees everyone the possibility of expressing

Jacques Chirac served for 12 years as the president of France (1995–2007) and sought legislation that banned the headscarf in French schools, as he felt that it threatened the secularity of the state.

© Langevin Jacques/Corbis Sygma

and practicing their faith, peacefully and freely, without the threat of the imposition of other convictions or beliefs. It allows women and men from all corners of the globe, from all cultures, to be protected in their beliefs by the Republic and its institutions. . . .

Like all freedoms, freedom of expression of religious beliefs can be limited only by the freedom of the other and observance of the rules of life in society. Religious freedom, which our country respects and protects, cannot be hijacked. It cannot undermine the common rule. It cannot impinge on the freedom of conviction of others. It is this subtle, precious and fragile balance, patiently built up over decades, which respect for the principle of secularism ensures. And this principle is an opportunity for France. This is why it is set down in Article 1 of our Constitution. This is why it is not negotiable! . . .

We must also reaffirm secularism at school, because school must be completely protected. School is first and foremost the place where the values bequeathed to us all are acquired and passed on. The instrument par excellence for entrenching the republican idea . . . school is a republican sanctuary which we must defend. . . . To protect our children, so that our youngsters are not exposed to divisive ill winds, which drive people apart and set them against one another. . . .

In all conscience, I consider that the wearing of clothes or signs which conspicuously denote a religious affiliation must be prohibited at school. Discreet signs, for example a cross, a Star of David or Hand of Fatima,* will of course remain allowed. On the other hand, conspicuous signs, i.e., those which stand out and immediately denote religious affiliation, must not be tolerated. These—the Islamic veil, regardless of the name you give it, the Kippa, or a cross of a clearly excessive size—have no place in state schools. State schools will remain secular. . . . It is to make the young people involved understand what is at stake and protect them from influences and passions which, far from liberating them or allowing them to make free choices, constrain or threaten them. . . . On the other hand—and the question has been raised—I do not think it necessary to add new national holidays to the school calendar, which already has many. . . .

I very solemnly proclaim: the Republic will oppose everything which divides, everything which discourages participation, and everything which excludes! The rule is "everyone together" because this places everyone on an equal footing, because it refuses to distinguish on the grounds of sex, origin, colour or religion.[3]

Muslim leaders protested the law as an attack on their religion, and demonstrations took place in France and in other countries. But within a year, the public row subsided. Reporter Adam Sage summarized its effect:

---

* The Hand of Fatima, or *Hamsah* (literally means "five" in Arabic and Hebrew), is a charm that looks like a human hand. The name refers to Fatima, the daughter of Muhammad. It is believed to bring good luck and to protect its owner from the "evil eye." See above for image.

> In the year since the law was implemented 626 girls have arrived for lessons wearing a Muslim headscarf—compared with 1,465 over the previous 12 months and more than 5,000 at the start of the decade. Of these, 496 agreed to remove them when summoned for a talk with the head teacher. A further 45 refused and were expelled.[4]

Many of these girls were placed in Catholic schools, which permit religious symbols. Others accepted the law. Sage interviewed Fathima, who was 16 in 2005. She said that she had learned to respect the law: "In the end I really don't think it was a bad law at all. I wear my *voile* until I get to the school gates and then I take it off. School is not a place for religion. It is a place where we are all French and we are all equal. After lessons, I put the scarf back on again. There's no difficulty."[5] Moreover, soon after the law went into effect, the so-called Islamic Army in Iraq kidnapped two French journalists and demanded that President Jacques Chirac overturn the ban if he wished to spare their lives. The Muslim population was united in condemning these actions and called for the unconditional release of the hostages. But while the protest against the law subsided, the social unrest in the *banlieues* did not.

On the evening of October 27, 2005, the police attempted to stop a group of French Muslim teenagers who were playing soccer in a field next to high-rise projects in Clichy-sous-Bois (one of the poorest *banlieue* neighborhoods near Paris). Though no crime was committed, a deadly chase ensued, and two young French Muslims who scaled an electrical substation were electrocuted.[6] News of the deaths spread rapidly via text messages, cell phones, and chat rooms. Sporadic clashes that started in Clichy-sous-Bois quickly spread to the nearby suburbs, then to nearby towns, and finally to all major cities across the country. Over the next two weeks, fires raged across France's suburbs, leaving behind a trail of charred cars, shopping centers, police stations, schools, and other symbols of the French state.

In 2005, the deaths of two French North Africans sparked over two weeks of violence across France. Rioters protested perceived systemic injustice and racism.

© Victor Tonelli/Reuters/Corbis

Connections

1. Why did President Chirac think that public schools must be protected from the influence of religion?

2. What does the phrase "ostentatious signs of religious proselytism" mean? Why did President Chirac think that such signs were splitting French society into separate communities?

3. What did the law achieve? What did it fail to achieve? How did the Muslim population respond to it?

4. Anthropologist John Bowen suggests that there were other ways for French schools to respond to the veil. He asks, "When girls of fourteen or seventeen try out . . . a new appearance, what does developmental psychology suggest is the best response? How did a girl's peers respond when she appeared with her head covered?" What do Bowen's questions add to the conversation? What factors does he hope politicians will consider when they respond to the veil?

[1] Paul A. Silverstein, "Headscarves and the French Tricolor," the *Middle East Reports* website, January 30, 2004, *http://www.merip.org/mero/mero013004.html* (accessed April 23, 2008).

[2] Jon Henley, "Something Aggressive About Veils, Says Chirac," the *Guardian* (December 6, 2003), *http://www.guardian.co.uk/france/story/0,11882,1101321,00.html* (accessed March 20, 2007).

[3] Jacques Chirac, "Principle of Secularism in the Republic" (speech, Paris, France, December 17, 2003), Embassy of France in the United States website, *http://www.info-france-usa.org/news/statmnts/2003/chirac_secularism121703.asp* (accessed November 27, 2007). The teaching week—much like the workweek—and the holidays in France follow the Christian calendar.

[4] Adam Sage, "Headscarf Ban Is Judged Success as Hostility Fades," the *Times Online* (September 5, 2005), *www.timesonline.co.uk/tol/news/world/europe/article562622.ece* (accessed January 3, 2008).

[5] Ibid.

[6] Molly Moore, "Anger Erupts in Paris Suburb after Deaths of Muslim Boys; Teenagers Were Electrocuted While Trying to Avoid Police," the *Washington Post*, November 2, 2005, *http://www.washingtonpost.com/wp-dyn/content/article/2005/11/01/AR2005110101761.html* (accessed November 27, 2007); Thomas Crampton, "Behind the Furor, the Last Moments of Two Youths," the *New York Times*, November 7, 2005, *http://www.nytimes.com/2005/11/07/international/europe/07youths.html/partner/rssnyt?ex=1164949200&en=3fbda36a57bfd0e3&ei=5070* (accessed November 27, 2007).

Europeans Debating the Veil

"We are certainly not trying to stamp out multiculturalism. But we are very anxious that the conflicts of the world are not brought into the classrooms."
– *Belgian Senator Alain Destexhe*

"Why, then, pay so much attention to French *laïcité*, which until now seemed to be an exception?" asks Olivier Roy, a leading French scholar on Islam.[1] He argues that the reason is that "there is today a convergence of the various debates taking place in Western countries: tellingly, they focus on the veil worn by some Muslim women."[2] What started in France in 1989, he suggests, continued over the next few years in the United Kingdom, the Netherlands, and many other European countries.

Three issues frame the debate about the veil in Europe. First, some Europeans feel that their historic Christian identity is being threatened by the growing presence of Islam in Europe. Second, fear of Islamic extremism is widespread, especially since the terrorist attacks in New York, Madrid, and London, which made that fear painfully real. Finally, many across the political spectrum worry that Europe's secular culture is undermined by Islam.

In these discussions, veils have also been linked to fears of Islamic extremism. In arguing for a ban on the veil, Italian politician Daniela Santanche explained that in Italy, "there is a law which forbids—for fear of terrorism—people to go around with masks on."[3] For similar reasons, Vice-Premier Francesco Rutelli of Italy called for the banning of the *niqab* in public, and Romano Prodi, then the Italian prime minister, declared that, beyond security issues, such a ban would be "important for society and for integration."[4] Although only a small number of women wear the *burqa* in the Netherlands (and in Europe in general), the country banned the wearing of the full-body cover because politicians claimed, among other things, that these garments could be used to hide explosives.

Despite debate on the issue, legislators in the United Kingdom recently decided against a ban on headscarves in publicly funded schools. Here Muslim students integrate their headscarves into their uniforms at a school in London.

© Gideon Mendel/Corbis

In Britain, several politicians have recently called for limitations on the use of the veil in public. Those arguments have been less religious than cultural. Echoing President Chirac's speech, Jack Straw, a member of the British parliament and a prominent cabinet member, explained that the facial veil made him uncomfortable and got in the way of communication. For Straw the veil is a sign of separateness, which can lead to the splitting of society into two "parallel communities"—one Muslim, the other European.[5] A second veil controversy heated up in Britain when a Muslim teacher was dismissed, in part, because she wore a *niqab* in the classroom.

Of all the factors shaping the debate about the veil, the need to preserve secularity is the one that drew the widest support. Following the decision to ban "ostentatious" religious symbols in France's public schools, Belgian Senator Alain Destexhe proposed a similar bill for his country. The concern, again, was primarily about creating neutral spaces for students to learn:

> We are certainly not trying to stamp out multiculturalism. But we are very anxious that the conflicts of the world are not brought into the classrooms, and that is why we support the French legislation and are trying to introduce a similar law in Belgium. For one, public spaces should be neutral spaces, not places to spread a particular view of the world. Secondly, we have a duty of care to children who enter the public school system, and there is certainly an issue that young Muslim women are often forced into wearing the headscarf by those around them.
>
> Therefore while some allege that we are taking away their individual freedoms, in some cases we will actually be restoring them. We want individuals to be integrated, and we want Muslim women to be viewed and treated as equals. . . . [N]obody is seeking to regulate what people do in their private sphere. . . . [We merely require] that in the public sphere, certain rules must apply. And it is better that these decisions are taken by a democratically elected government, than leaving the matter to individual schools to decide upon.[6]

At present, decisions about the veil in Belgium are left to individual schools. The veil has also presented a major challenge to left-wing political activists in Europe who traditionally see themselves as advocates of minority rights. For many feminists, the issue of the veil became one of women's rights. For example, Alice Schwarzer, a prominent German feminist, argues that

> [t]his issue is about the constitution, and the [separation] between state and religion—a hard fought achievement of the [E]nlightenment. . . . The passiveness of politicians leaves the majority of Muslim women in Germany powerless against the militant minority of fundamentalists.[7]

But voices supporting religious expression of the veil are also heard in Europe. In a 2005 ruling about school uniform policy, the British court of appeals upheld students' right of religious expression. The court explained that school uniform policies must "start with the premise that a student had a right to manifest her religious beliefs."[8] This position is anchored in the United Kingdom's Human Rights Act of 1998, which states that "Everyone has the right to . . . manifest [their] religion or belief, in worship, teaching, practice and observance."[9] While there are no national policies either upholding or forbidding students to wear the veil in school, the National Union of Teachers developed its own guidelines for creating inclusive school uniform policies. These explained:

> When drawing up a school uniform policy it is important that the governing body identifies clearly the purpose to be achieved by its introduction. Alongside identification of the purpose of the policy, must lie the recognition that in principle, pupils have a right to dress in accordance with the requirements of their religious beliefs. It should be recognized that for Muslims in particular, the concepts of modesty and dignity in dress carry the status of religious obligation.
>
> Though there may be differences in interpretation of the requirement of modesty of dress among Muslims, schools should:
>
> - generally avoid making assumptions about how this modesty is best expressed;
> - enable individual choice to be exercised within a broad dress code framework;
> - seek to avoid privileging one interpretation of the requirement for modesty of dress of one group of parents and pupils over another interpretation by a different set of parents; and
> - consider carefully whether it would be appropriate for their school uniform policy to override the beliefs of some Muslims whilst permitting other Muslims to adhere to a different dress code of their choice.
>
> When considering, in more detail, how to accommodate the different cultural and religious needs of pupils within a single school uniform policy, a basic starting point for the discussion might therefore be the question of whether a pupil's choice of dress hinders the process of *teaching and learning*. Within the context of teaching and learning, issues ranging from ensuring equal access to the curriculum to the relationship between pupils and between pupils and teachers might be examined.[10]

Veil Regulations in Several Western European Countries[11]

Country	Regulations
France	The *hijab* is banned in public schools.
Netherlands	Parliament pushes to ban the wearing of the *burqa*. Currently in discussions in the government.
Norway	The *niqab* is banned in schools in Oslo.
Sweden	Individual schools can decide to ban *niqab/burqa*. National Agency for Education upholds the right to wear a veil.
United Kingdom	Several ministers and members of parliament expressed concerns about the wearing of the veil in public, which causes a debate about the full-face covering (*niqab* or *burka*).

Connections

1. Why do you think the veil has become the center of so much controversy?

2. What kinds of religious practices can governments ask people to give up in order to create a harmonious community?

3. How can people express their religious commitment in a secular society? When do religious commitments and secular values come into conflict?

4. What kinds of cultural practices should people be willing to give up in order to assimilate? At what point does assimilation threaten a group's cultural identity?

5. Compare the policy recommendations from the National Union of Teachers with French Prime Minister Chirac's speech in the reading *Europeans Debating the Veil*. What assumptions does each make about religion, identity, and integration?

6. How can educators reconcile the need to treat people equally, the need to treat people differently, and the need to cultivate a shared sense of belonging?

---

[1] Olivier Roy, *Secularism Confronts Islam*, trans. George Holoch (New York: Columbia University Press, 2007), xii.

[2] Ibid.

[3] Christian Fraser, "Protection for Italy Veil Row MP," *BBC News*, October 23, 2006, *http://news.bbc.co.uk/2/hi/europe/6078392.stm* (accessed November 27, 2007).

[4] Christian Fraser, "Italy Government Seeks Veil Ban," *BBC News*, November 7, 2006, *http://news.bbc.co.uk/2/hi/europe/6125302.stm* (accessed November 27, 2007).

[5] "'Remove full veils' urges Straw," *BBC News*, October 6, 2007, *http://news.bbc.co.uk/2/hi/uk_news/politics/5411954.stm* (accessed November 27, 2007).

[6] "Viewpoints: Europe and the Headscarf," *BBC News*, February 10, 2004, *http://news.bbc.co.uk/2/hi/europe/3459963.stm#Alain* (accessed November 27, 2007).

[7] Ibid.

[8] The National Union of Teachers, *The Muslim Faith and School Uniform: Wearing the Hijab and Other Islamic Dress in Schools* (London: The National Union of Teachers, 2006), *http://www.religionlaw.co.uk/reportcd.pdf* (accessed April 24, 2008), 5.

[9] Human Rights Act 1998 (c. 42), Article 9, Office of Public Sector Information website, *http://www.opsi.gov.uk/ACTS/acts1998/ukpga_19980042_en_3* (accessed April 25, 2008).

[10] The National Union of Teachers, *The Muslim Faith and School Uniform*, 6.

Glossary

antisemitism: "Antisemitism is a certain perception of Jews, which may be expressed as hatred toward Jews. . . . Antisemitism frequently charges Jews with conspiring to harm humanity, and it is often used to blame Jews for 'why things go wrong.' It is expressed in speech, writing, visual forms and action, and employs sinister stereotypes and negative character traits" (The European Monitoring Centre on Racism and Xenophobia).[1]

assimilation: A process through which immigrants accept the national culture of the host country and give up their group identity. France is said to favor a strong assimilation model.

les affaires du foulard ("veil affairs" in French)**:** A series of public debates about the right of Muslim girls to wear the Islamic veil to school in France. The first "veil affair" occurred in 1989. In 2003, Islamic veils (and other big religious symbols) were banned in public schools.

babouches: Traditional Moroccan slippers.

banlieues: Suburbs on the outskirts of large cities in France where, in many cases, the majority of the population are North African immigrants. Many areas in these neighborhoods are marked by poverty, very high unemployment rates, black markets, and crime.

Beurs: The name second-generation immigrants of Arab descent gave themselves. *Beur* is the inversion of the sounds and syllables in *Arabe* ("Arab" in French)—an example of the French slang called *Verlan* (see separate entry). The word *Beurs* has a positive connotation, while the term *Arabe* is often derogatory.

burqa: An Arabic word describing a full-body veil. It covers the entire face and body, and the woman who wears it sees through a mesh screen that covers her eyes. It is most commonly worn in Afghanistan and Pakistan. Under the Taliban regime in Afghanistan (1996–2001), its use was mandated by law.

chador: A Persian word describing a full-length shawl held at the neck by hand or pin. It covers the head and the body but leaves the face visible. *Chadors* are most often black and are common in Iran, where, since the Islamic Revolution of 1979, they have been mandatory for all women.

compulsory education: Education required by law for all students under a specific age. The Jules Ferry Laws of 1881–1882 and 1886 made primary education compulsory for boys and girls in France. These laws also banished religion as a subject and priests and nuns as teachers from classrooms in public schools.

djellaba: A Moroccan Arabic word for a traditional garment that is worn widely in many Arab regions. It has loose, long sleeves and a long skirt that can be worn by either sex.

egalité: French word meaning "equality." This principle became part of the motto *"liberté, égalité, fraternité"* that represented the new French Republic during the French Revolution (1789–1799).

Enlightenment (also known as the Age of Reason)**:** An eighteenth-century European intellectual movement that influenced many democratic movements. Among its tenets are the ideas that reason, science, and education can lead humanity to freedom and material progress; that since all humans are endowed with reason, they are capable of self-government; and that since many religious claims aren't based on reason or science, they are largely false.

emancipation: The granting of civic and political rights to groups or individuals (hence "liberating" them). The modern use of the term is associated with granting civic rights to religious minorities, such as the Catholics and, especially, the Jews in eighteenth- and nineteenth-century Europe.

fatwa: An Arabic word for a legal decree or declaration made by a Muslim religious leader.

fraternité: French for "brotherhood." The term, which emphasizes the solidarity and connection between all French citizens, was attributed to the French Revolution (1789–1799) in the nineteenth century. It became part of the revolutionary three-part motto *"liberté, égalité, fraternité."*

fundamentalism: Strict adherence to the literal words of an ancient text that is believed to be true (the Bible or the Quran, for example). While some fundamentalists seek to impose the principles and laws found in such texts on everybody (and sometimes even resort to violence), most fundamentalists live peacefully among their neighbors and respect the separation of state and church.

genocide: A term coined by Raphael Lemkin to describe mass crimes directed against national, religious, or ethnic groups. To qualify as genocide, Lemkin argued, these crimes must be "directed against individuals, not in their individual capacity, but as members of the national group."[2]

globalization: The increasing flow of people, ideas, commodities, languages, and traditions throughout the world. Modern transportation, migration, e-business, multi-national companies, and trade agreements, as well as the use of the Internet and cell phones, speeds up this process and contributes to a "global culture," which some fear threatens the diversity of human cultures.

guest worker: A category of workers who enter a country legally in order to work and are expected to leave after their visas expire. Following World War II, France recruited hundreds of thousands of guest workers from former colonies in North Africa to aid in its booming economy. Many of them stayed and made France their home.

Hadith: Reports by eyewitnesses, experts, and companions of the prophet Muhammad. Originally part of an oral tradition, these reports help different Islamic schools interpret the words, intentions, and actions of the founder of Islam.

hijab: Originating from the Arabic word for "curtain," it is a veil (*voile* in French) worn by many Muslim women in observance of their faith. *Hijab* is a means of preserving one's modesty, as well as a display of cultural affiliation and religious devotion. The *hijab* is one name for a variety of similar headscarves that cover the head and neck, and often the hair and forehead; the style, shape, and color are the choice of the wearer.

inalienable rights: Originating from the Enlightenment movement, this phrase refers to rights to which all humans are entitled—rights that cannot be taken away from them under any circumstances. These rights are defined, for example, in the American Declaration of Independence of 1776 ("life, liberty, and the pursuit of happiness") and the French Declaration of the Rights of Man and Citizen of 1789 ("liberty, property, security, and resistance to oppression").

Islamists: Often described as fundamentalists, Islamists preach that Islam is not only a religion but also a social and political system that governs most aspects of life. The majority of Islamists attempt to replace secular attitudes and regulations in a peaceful manner, but a small minority of them resort to extreme measures, including violence and even terror.

kippah: Literally meaning "dome" or "mountaintop," *kippah* is the Hebrew word for a Jewish skullcap often worn by many Orthodox and other Jewish men as a sign of devotion and respect for God.

laïcité: French for "secularity." The term comes from the word *lay* or *laity*, which refers to Christians who did not belong to religious orders or to the clergy. Secularism is used to describe governments that maintain a separation of church and state. Countries such as France, which upholds this separation, ask believers to practice their religion for the most part in private. While generally the term refers to the neutrality of the state toward religious groups, some in France interpret it as the Republic's official culture.

liberté: French for "liberty." This term became part of the motto ("liberty, equality, brotherhood") representing the new French Republic during the French Revolution (1789–1799).

Maghreb: A region of North Africa where three former French colonies are located—Morocco, Algeria, and Tunisia. Maghrebian immigrants and their sons and daughters form a growing minority in France. In some urban centers, they make up the majority of the current population. These immigrants speak various dialects of the Arabic language and Kabyle, the language of the Berber or Kabyle people.

multiculturalism: An ideology and social policy that assumes that a society can have multiple cultural identities. In such a society, citizens maintain their group identity alongside their national identity. As an integration policy, multiculturalism attempts to create a two-way dialogue between the communities of newcomers (or minorities) and the rest of the population. In contrast, assimilation means that newcomers give up their minority's identity and are expected to blend in.

nationalism: A political ideology that emphasizes national culture or interests above those of minorities and other sub-national groups.

nation-states: A term describing most modern states, where members of a single (and, ideally, homogenous) nation inhabit a defined geographic area or a country. The creation of nation-states began in the nineteenth century, and this process of nation-building required the creation of national communication, transportation, and educational systems and the marginalization of regional cultural differences.

niqab: A *niqab* covers the entire body, head, and face; however, an opening is left for the eyes. The two main types of *niqab* are the half-*niqab* that consists of a headscarf and facial veil that leaves the eyes and part of the forehead visible, and the full, or Gulf, *niqab* that leaves only a narrow slit for the eyes. These veils are popular across the Muslim world, though they are most common in the Gulf states. Some politicians have argued for banning the *niqab*; some feel that it interferes with communication or creates security concerns.

Pasqua Law: Named after the French interior minister Charles Pasqua, this set of laws was enacted in 1993 in an effort to stem the immigration flow into France.

pluralism: The term refers to the belief that diversity is an asset to a society. See also: *multiculturalism.*

popular sovereignty: The belief that the people of a state should freely choose their state's government and that no government can rule against the will of the people. The French Republic following the French Revolution of 1789 was founded on the principle of popular sovereignty.

Quran: The holy book of the Islamic faith.

Ramadan: An Arabic word for the ninth month of the lunar calendar. During an entire month, observant Muslims pray, atone for their sins, perform acts of charity, fast from sunrise to sunset, and celebrate the revelation of the Quran to the prophet Muhammad. The month ends with Eid ul-Fitr—a three-day holiday that breaks the fasting period.

secularity: See *laïcité.*

stigmatization: Negatively labeling a person or a group based solely on assumptions and stereotypes. Stigmatization is the result of prejudices, fears, or other negative feelings toward this person or group (for example, assuming that a Muslim headscarf signifies that the wearer believes in fundamentalism or radicalism).

Verlan: The inversion of sounds and syllables in a word to create a new word. The word *Beur* as a substitute for the word *Arab* is an example. The word *verlan* itself was created by inverting the two syllables in the French word *envers*, which means "backward." It is a form of slang very typical of the *banlieues.*

xenophobia: Fear and hatred of foreigners or immigrants. It comes from the Greek words *xenos*, meaning "foreigner" or "stranger," and *phobos*, meaning "fear."

[1] "Working Definition of Antisemitism," The European Union Agency for Fundamental Rights website, *http://fra.europa.eu/fra/material/pub/AS/AS-WorkingDefinition-draft.pdf* (accessed September 8, 2008).

[2] Raphael Lemkin, *Axis Rule in Occupied Europe, Laws of Occupation, Analysis of Government, Proposals for Redress* (Washington: Carnegie Endowment for World Peace, 1944), 79.